BEGINNING WITH THE BIBLE

A CLASS ABOVE

a child's further lessons
in knowing God

The Old Testament

TnT Ministries

CHRISTIAN FOCUS PUBLICATIONS

TnT Ministries (which stands for Teaching and Training) was launched in February 1993 by Christians from a broad variety of denominational backgrounds who are concerned that teaching the Bible to children be taken seriously. They have been in charge of the Sunday School of 50 teachers at St Helen's Bishopsgate, an evangelical church in the City of London, for 13 years, during which time a range of Biblical teaching materials has been developed. TnT Ministries also runs training days for Sunday School teachers.

© TnT Ministries
29 Buxton Gardens, Acton, London, W3 9LE
Tel: +44 (0) 181 992 0450 Fax: +44 (0) 181 896 1847

Published in 1999 by Christian Focus Publications Ltd.
Geanies House, Fearn, Tain, Ross-shire, IV20 1TW
Tel: +44 (0) 1862 871 011 Fax: +44 (0) 1862 871 699

Cover design by Douglas McConnach

ISBN 1-85792-454-1

All Scripture references are from the Good News Bible except where indicated.

Contents

Contributors: Trevor and Thalia Blundell, Monica Farthing, Rachel Garforth-Bles, Annie Gemmill, Kathy Manchester, Hilary Nash

Artist: Andrew Blundell

Beginning with the Bible

Old Testament Bible Lessons for Young Children

Beginning with the Bible is a series of lessons designed to teach small children the main Bible stories. It is a sequel to *First Class*, which introduces young children to basic concepts about God and his world.
Beginning with the Bible consists of two books, one covering stories from the Old Testament and one from the New. This book contains 25 lessons, covering creation to Jonah, plus a twenty-sixth that can be slotted in when there are 53 Sundays in the year. There are a further 2 lessons that can be used if Easter is early.

Beginning with the Bible can be used anywhere where there are 2½ - 4 year old children - at home, in a play group or church crèche. The lessons can be taught by parents or anyone else who has the care of young children, without any special teacher training being required.

Why teach young children Bible stories?

Children of this age have already demonstrated their remarkable capacity to learn. They love stories and are quick to identify with what they hear. They are able to enjoy loving relationships with parents and other significant adults. They also have the ability to develop a simple trust in God.

We believe that the Bible is God's word to mankind, and that it contains everything we need to know in order to be reconciled with God and live in a way that is pleasing to him. Therefore, we believe it is vital to teach small children what God has to say, so that they can learn who he is and what he has done. We need to lay a foundation of knowledge about God that will enable them to develop a relationship with him and grow into Christian maturity in later years.

How do young children learn?

Children in the 2½ - 4 year old age bracket cover a broad range of abilities. Many of them will attend a play group or nursery class, so will be used to other children.

They love to practise skills and learn mainly by repetition.

Most children of this age will have a good basic vocabulary, but care needs to be taken to use appropriate language. Words should be simple and sentences short and the teacher needs to avoid Christian jargon, e.g. small children do not understand the word *sin*, but easily identify with *all the naughty things I do*. Do remember that children in this age group are full of questions and learn through exploration and involvement.

Visually, young children love bright colours and simple images. Therefore, pictures used in teaching sessions must be big, clearly drawn and uncluttered. At the younger end of the age range hand/eye co-ordination is at an early stage, so colouring in tends to come out as a scribble, whereas many 4 year olds are able to produce a creditable effort. Do remember that girls develop skills earlier than boys. Even though the end result may look disastrous the children still enjoy it and can take pride in what they have created. They cannot use scissors, but are able to glue with help.

Children enjoy making things to keep or take home that remind them of what has been learned, even if they have had very little part in their making. Therefore, much of the craft work outlined in the lessons needs to be prepared in advance of the time when you are teaching the children in class.

Children of this age have a short attention span (5-7 minutes maximum) and the lessons are designed with this in mind. Therefore, it is important to choose a suitable time for the teaching. The children need time to settle down after parents have left, but still be fresh enough to listen and learn. In order to gain maximum benefit from the session there needs to be 1 adult for every 3-4 children. Opportunities for reinforcing the lesson should be found during play time.

How to use this book

The lessons have been designed so that they can be used at home or as a short slot in a longer session. They can be taught as an interlude in a church crèche or play group, or at home on a Sunday afternoon or other convenient time of the week.

Each lesson is set out in the same way. The title is followed by the **Lesson aim**, which details what the child is expected to learn from that particular session. This is followed by a section entitled **Preparation**, which sets out the Bible passage for the story, with some questions to help you think about what the story is teaching. This bit is easy to skip, but for the sake of the children and yourself please be committed to making adequate spiritual preparation, as well as preparing the visual aids and craft work. To prepare a lesson properly takes 2-3 hours.

The next section consists of a detailed **Lesson plan**, which must be thoroughly understood and learned, so that the children can be taught without reference to the lesson material. The Bible story is written out in suitable language as a guide only; it should **not** be read to the children. This section includes ideas for visual aids and 2 or 3 activities to help reinforce the lesson.

Give time to teaching the children, letting them contribute and ask questions, but keep it as short as possible, otherwise their attention will wander and the opportunity be lost. Try to strike a balance between the lesson being fun, and yet serious. Your attitude is very important - they will take their lead from you.

Remember always to check activities and crafts for potential **safety** problems. Although every care has been taken in the preparation of this material to avoid safety hazards, you need to be aware of possible problems in the class area for the children. This age group can be very boisterous!

Each lesson ends with a **Prayer**. Although we sometimes find the idea of prayer difficult to understand, for children it is often very natural. Closing eyes and holding hands together is not necessary, but it helps them to concentrate. Young children find a prayer drill helpful, done to a count of 3, e.g.
1. shake your hands out in front,
2. bring your hands together in front,
3. bring your hands up to your chest and close your eyes.

Try to get them to understand that God is listening and wants to hear our prayers. Many children of this age will be happy to pray out loud and this should be encouraged. Never force any child to pray.

At the back of the book you will find details of how to make some of the suggested **Visual aids**.

What results?

We believe that, carefully and prayerfully used, these lessons will lay a foundation of Bible knowledge that will result in the child learning who God is and what he has done. As with **First Class**, we hope that **Beginning with the Bible** will result in:

1. The child developing a simple trust in God.
2. The parents learning to be relaxed, natural and confident in teaching their child from the Bible.
3. The child entering Sunday School/Junior Church ready to learn and take part in a more traditional lesson.
4. The teacher growing in his/her own relationship with God. You cannot teach even a 3 year old something you do not fully understand!

Teaching small children is an important job and is worth doing well, even though it is time-consuming if done properly. Jesus said: *'Let the little children come to me, and do not hinder them, for the kingdom of God belongs to such as these.'* (Luke 18:16). If Jesus thought children important, who are we to deny them access to his word which brings life?

Creation

> **Lesson aim:** to teach that God made everything and it was good.

Preparation

1. Read Genesis 1:1 - 2:3.

2. Think about the way God made the world:
   - God made everything (v.1),
   - he made it from nothing (v.1-2),
   - he made it by feeding the information in (using his word - vv.3,6,9,11,14,20,24,26),
   - he made it in stages,
   - it was all good (v.31).

3. Pray for the children you teach, asking God to help them understand that he made everything and it was good.

4. Choose appropriate visual aids.

To-day we are going to learn how the world was made.

When God first made the world it was dark and empty. Then God said, *'Let there be light.'* God called the light Day, and the dark Night. And it was good. That was the first day.

On the second day God made the sky and it was good.

On the third day God separated the land from the sea. And God made all the plants - the trees and their fruit, the flowers, and the grass. And they were all good.

On the fourth day God made the sun to shine by day, and the moon and the stars to shine by night. And they were good.

On the fifth day God made the fish to swim in the sea, and the birds to fly in the air. And they were good.

On the sixth day God made all the animals - (Ask the children to name animals as they are stuck in place). And right at the end God made a man called Adam, and a woman called Eve. And God saw that it was all very good.

And on the seventh day God rested.

Prayer

Dear God, thank you for making a lovely world for us to live in. Amen.

Visual aids

Pictures from a Child's Story Bible.

Activities

1. Give each child a sheet of coloured paper on the bottom of which is written, *God saw all that he had made, and it was very good. Genesis 1:31.*
   Either make cut-outs of sun, moon, stars, birds, fish, etc. from coloured sticky paper (see page 8), or cut pictures out of magazines. Place a set of cut-outs in an envelope for each child. The children stick them onto the paper.

2. Make a creation booklet with each child. This activity takes more time than activity 1 but makes the stages of creation clearer.
   Fold 2 A4 pieces of paper in half to make a booklet of 8 pages. Staple at the join.
   Write *Creation* plus the Bible verse from activity 1 on the front page. Name the remaining pages from Day 1 to Day 7. On Day 1 draw a big circle to represent the world and draw a line across the centre of the circle.
   Either make cut-outs of sun, moon, stars, birds, fish, etc. from coloured sticky paper (see page 8), or cut pictures out of magazines. Place a set of cut-outs in an envelope for each child.
   Make the booklet with the children. They can colour in the light and dark sections on Day 1 and then glue the pictures in the appropriate places in the rest of the booklet.

The Fall

Lesson aim: to teach that sin puts a barrier between me and God.

Preparation

1. Read Genesis 2:15-17; 3:1-24.

2. Answer the following questions:
   - was work a product of the Fall? (2:15-17)
   - were Adam and Eve aware of God's prohibition regarding the tree of the knowledge of good and evil? (2:16-17; 3:2-3)
   - did Eve quote God's word accurately? (3:3)
   - why did Eve listen to the serpent rather than God? (3:6)
   - how did sin affect Adam and Eve's relationship with each other (3:7) and with God (3:8)?
   - did their sin result in death, as 'God said? (2:16-17; 3:22-24)

3. Note the following:
   - Satan encouraged Eve to doubt God's word (3:1).
   - Eve added to God's word (3:2-3).
   - Satan denied the doctrine of judgment (3:4).
   - Satan encouraged Eve to doubt God's goodness and made her want to be like God (3:5).
   - both tried to shift the blame (3:12-13).
   - the first glimpse of the gospel (3:15). Jesus was the offspring of the woman who would crush Satan at the cross.
   - only God could provide a covering for Adam and Eve's shame (3:21 cf. 3:10).
   - God's kindness in not allowing man to live for ever in a state of separation from God (3:22-24). Death must enter the world if God is to provide a remedy for man's sin.

4. Ask God to help you teach this story clearly and sensitively.

5. Choose appropriate visual aids.

Children of this age are not embarrassed by nudity, so it can be confusing to mention the garments of vine leaves. Start by reminding the children of last week's story - Creation. Ask them to name some of the things that God made. Remind them that everything was good when God made it. Ask them if they are always good. Do they ever do naughty things. Point out that everyone does naughty things, even their parents and teachers. In today's story from the Bible we will find out why we do naughty things.

After God made the man, Adam, and the woman, Eve, he gave them a lovely big garden to live in. God told them to look after the garden and everything in it. It was a lovely garden and Adam and Eve did not need to wear any clothes.

There were lots of trees in this garden with beautiful fruit to eat. But there was one tree that God said, *'Don't eat this fruit or you will die.'*

One day Eve was near this tree when a big snake spoke to her. He said that she should disobey God and eat the fruit from the forbidden tree (point to it). Eve listened to the snake. She picked the fruit and ate it. And then she gave some to Adam and he ate it.

That evening, when God came to the garden, Adam and Eve hid from him, for they were afraid. God called to them and asked them what they had done. They told God that they had disobeyed him and eaten the forbidden fruit.

God was angry. He sent them away from the garden. But God still loved them. He made Adam and Eve warm clothes from animal skins. After Adam and Eve had left the garden, God made a barrier to stop them coming back.

Finish by stating that, since the time of Adam and Eve, everyone has done naughty things (except Jesus).

Prayer

Dear God, thank you for loving me, even when I do naughty things. Amen.

Visual aids

Pictures from a Child's Story Bible.

Activities

1. Photocopy this page back to back with page 11 for each child. Cut around the line above the text and fold along the dotted line.
   The children colour the picture of Adam and Eve by the forbidden tree. When the bottom part of the page is folded up they can be seen hiding from God behind a bush. The folded-up portion can be coloured green.

2. Make a walled garden from lego or similar. This should be done as a joint activity. Build a wall around the garden with with one entrance. If you have lego trees use them, otherwise make trees beforehand from pipe cleaners and green paper. Stick the trees to the base with bluetak. When the garden is finished designate one of the trees as the tree of life and another as the tree of the knowledge of good and evil. Go over the story using a question and answer format. Put a barrier across the entrance after Adam and Eve have been sent out of the garden.

Adam and Eve disobeyed God.

When they heard God coming,
they hid from him.

God sent them away from his garden.

Adam and Eve lived in God's garden.

God said: 'Do not eat the fruit from the tree in the middle of the garden.'

Lesson 3

The Flood

> **Lesson aim: to show that God hates sin, but has made a way of escape for those who obey him.**

Preparation

1. Read Genesis 6:5 - 8:22; 9:8-17.

2. Answer the following questions:
   - how many people went into the ark? (6:10,17)
   - how many of each kind of creature went into the ark? (6:19-20; 7:2-3)
   - what were the clean animals? (Leviticus 11)
   - who shut the door (7:16)
   - what does the rainbow signify? (9:8-17)

A long time ago, there lived a man called Noah. Noah and all his family loved God. Noah did what God told him to do.

But the other people in the world did not love God. They were mean and selfish. (Talk about the sort of things the people did, e.g. fighting, stealing, etc.) This made God sad, and angry too, because they were spoiling the earth he had made.

God told Noah that he was going to send a flood to cover the whole earth. (You may need to explain 'flood'.) All the animals, birds and people would die. But God would save Noah and all his family.

Then God told Noah how to make a big boat called an ark. Noah listened carefully. Then Noah made the ark just as God told him to.

When the ark was finished Noah collected every kind of bird and animal to go in the ark too. God told Noah how many of each kind of animal and bird to take into the ark. Noah took 7 pairs of every kind of bird, 7 pairs of some animals and 1 pair of other animals, just as God told him.

When they were all safely inside, God shut the door. Then the rain came. It rained, and rained, and rained and rained. Soon there was water everywhere. The water covered all the trees and all the mountains. The ark bobbed up and down for days and days. Finally God stopped the rain and the water began to

go down. Then the ark landed on a mountain. Noah, his family, all the animals and all the birds came out.

Then Noah said thank you to God for keeping them safe.

As he did, God put the first rainbow in the sky to tell them and us that he would never flood the whole world again.

Prayer

Dear God, thank you for saving Noah's family and the birds and animals. Thank you that you have promised never to flood the earth again. Amen.

Visual aids

Pictures from a Child's Story Bible.

Activities

1. Photocopy page 13 for each child.
   Prior to the lesson, fold the page in half along the dotted lines and cut around the shape of the ark.
   Cut along the unbroken lines around the door and window and fold back along the dotted lines.
   The children colour the ark and the animals.
   The animals appear in the door and window when opened.
   Ask the children if they can remember the things that Noah did which God told him to do.

2. Designate an area of the room to be the ark. Mark the boundaries in some way, e.g. with a rope on the floor, masking tape, etc. Divide the children into pairs and tell them which animal or bird each pair is. The teacher takes the part of Noah and rounds up the animals and birds to go into the ark. The children make appropriate animal noises, flap their arms if they are birds, etc.

3. Make a mural to put on the wall.
   You need a length of plain wallpaper or large sheet of paper with a big rainbow drawn on it, animals, birds, people and scenery cut from magazines, and a cut-out of an ark.
   The children colour the rainbow and background appropriately. Glue the cut-outs onto the background to show what happened after the flood waters receded.

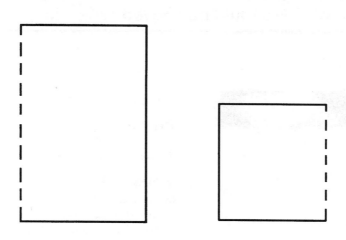

Noah did all that the Lord
commanded him.
Genesis 7:5

God Chooses Abraham

Lesson aim: to teach that God is trustworthy and should be obeyed.

Preparation

1. Read Genesis 12:1-7.

2. Answer the following questions:
   - where was Abraham living? (11:27-32)
   - how would Abraham know when he got to the right land?
   - what did God promise Abraham?
   - how would Abraham be a blessing to the nations? (Galatians 3:6-9)

3. Abraham demonstrated his trust in God by obedience. Think about how you can teach the children the importance of doing what God says, without implying that obedience is the way to be God's friend.

4. Pray for the children, asking God to help you teach them about his trustworthiness.

5. Choose and prepare appropriate visual aids.

Remind the children of previous lessons. Our story today is about a man who lived a long time after Noah. In those days a lot of people lived in big tents.

Make a tent to show the children how the people lived (see visual aids). Abraham was a man who lived a long time ago. He was a friend of God. One day God told Abraham that he wanted him to pack up all his things and move to another country.

Abraham did not know where this would be, but he knew he could trust God to know best. So, he packed up all his belongings, took his wife and all his animals and set off. Abraham knew that God was with them and would look after them.

Abraham and his party travelled a long way. At last they came to the place God had chosen. Then God promised Abraham that he would give this land to Abraham's family.

Stress the lesson aim at this point.

Prayer
Dear God, thank you for looking after Abraham. Thank you for looking after us too. Amen.

Visual aids
Models are a good way to show the children how Abraham would have lived.

For the tent you require a large piece of card for the base, 2 long pencils, 4 medium pencils, bluetak, a large piece of material and drawing pins.

Place the pencils stuck in bluetak on the base (see diagram). Drape the material over the top. Slit the material up the centre front to form the entrance flaps. Use 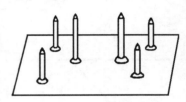 drawing pins to secure the bottom of the material to the card base.

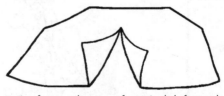

Make mats from pieces of material frayed at both ends. Make pots and bowls from playdough and leave to harden. (For playdough recipe see page 79.)

Having made the tent, set up the bed mats, pots, etc., showing them to the children as you do it.

Make Abraham and Sarah from peg people (see visual aids on page 78).

Use toy animals for Abraham's sheep, camels, cows, etc.

Activities
1. Photocopy the picture of Abraham on page 15 for each child. Trace the shape of his robe onto card to make a template and cut out a material robe for each child to glue onto the picture. The children can glue cotton wool onto Abraham's hair and beard.

2. Act out the story.

God told Abraham to take his family and everything he owned and move to another country, which God would show him.

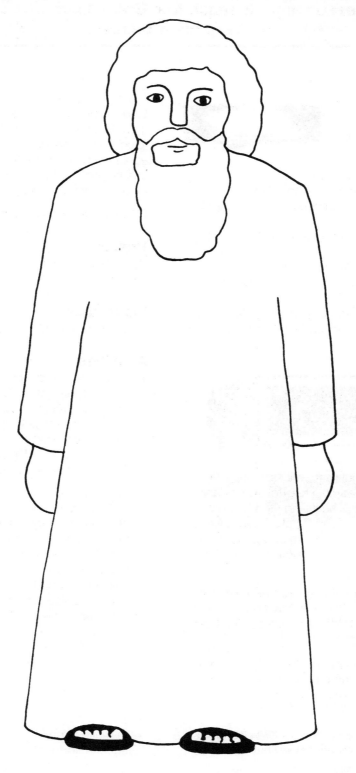

Abraham went, as the Lord had told him.
Genesis 12:4

Birth of Isaac

Lesson aim: to teach that God can be trusted to keep his promises.

Preparation

1. Read Genesis 15:1-6; 18:1-15; 21:1-7.

2. Answer the following questions:
   - what did God promise Abraham? (15:4)
   - why was Abraham righteous in God's sight? (15:6)
   - who appeared to Abraham? (18:1-2,16-18; 19:1)
   - why did Sarah laugh? (18:10-12)
   - how old was Abraham when Isaac was born? (21:5)
   - how many years had passed since God first promised Abraham descendants? (12:1-4)

Remind the children about last week's story - God choosing Abraham and leading him to a new land. After Abraham arrived in the new land God had given him, God promised that he and Sarah would have a son. Many years passed. Abraham and Sarah were now very old and still had no children. Had God forgotten his promise?

God showed Abraham the sky at night and told him to try and count the stars. *'Your family will be as many as the stars,'* God said. Abraham believed that God would do what he promised.

One day Abraham was sitting outside his tent. It was a very hot day. Suddenly he saw three men. *'Come and sit down and have something to eat and drink,'* Abraham told them.

After dinner, one of them said, *'Nine months from now I will come back and your wife Sarah will have a son'.*

Sarah was behind them (Point to Sarah in the tent). When she heard what the man said she laughed. She said, *'We are too old to have a baby!'* The man said to Abraham, *'Why did Sarah laugh? Nothing is too hard for God. In nine months I will come back, and Sarah will have a son.'*

God made Abraham and Sarah happy. He gave them a baby son as he had promised. Sarah said, *'God has made me so happy. Everyone who hears about my baby will be happy.'* She was so happy that she laughed. Abraham called the baby Isaac. Isaac means: 'someone laughs'.

Stress the lesson aim at this point.

Prayer
Dear God, thank you for always keeping your promises. Amen.

Visual aids
Pictures from a Child's Story Bible.

Activities
1. Each child requires 1 sheet of dark coloured paper (grey, dark blue or black), a figure of Abraham traced or photocopied from page 17, and silver and gold stars. Along the bottom of the paper write *'He who promised is faithful. Hebrews 10:23'.* The children glue on the figure of Abraham looking up at the stars.

2. Make a pendant. Photocopy page 17 for each child on card. Prior to the lesson cut out the circle and punch a hole at X. Thread a length of wool through the hole so that the card circle can hang round the child's neck. (Make sure that the wool is easily broken - danger of strangulation.) The children colour the figures of Abraham, Sarah and Isaac. Coloured stars can be stuck round the outer rim of the pendant.

Abraham and Sarah had a son, just as God had promised.

Joseph Sold by his Family

Lesson aim: to teach that sin spoils relationships and displeases God.

Preparation

1. Read Genesis 37:1-36.

2. Answer the following questions:
   - what relationship was Jacob to Abraham? (25:19-26)
   - who comprised Jacob's family and what were their relationships to each other? (29:16 - 30:24; 35:16-18)
   - why did Joseph's brothers hate him?
   - look at Joseph's actions (37:2,5,9). How would these have affected his relationship with his family?
   - how did Jacob treat Joseph?
   - what was wrong with the brothers' behaviour? (37:17-32)

3. Think about the family Joseph grew up in, with all its problems. Ask God to help you tell the story clearly and simply, so that the children understand the lesson aim. Be sensitive to the needs of any children with difficult home circumstances.

4. Choose appropriate visual aids.

Remind the children of last week's lesson - the birth of Isaac.

When Isaac grew up he had a son called Jacob. When Jacob grew up he had 12 sons. One of these was called Joseph. Jacob loved Joseph more than his other children. (Comment on this being a bad thing - parents love their children equally.)

Jacob made Joseph a special coat with long sleeves. Joseph's brothers didn't have special coats. They were very jealous.

Joseph had dreams about being the boss of his brothers. He told his brothers about the dreams. His brothers hated him.

One day Joseph's brothers were looking after the sheep and were a long way from home. Jacob sent Joseph to see what they were doing.

When Joseph got to the place where his brothers were, they grabbed hold of him and put him in a deep hole in the ground. Then they sat down to have their dinner.

Some people came past on their way to another country called Egypt. Joseph's brothers sold Joseph to these people to be a slave and they took him away to Egypt. But God looked after Joseph and next week we'll hear what happened in Egypt.

Discuss what happened with the children.
- Everyone did naughty things (itemise them).
- Did it make them happy?
- Did it make God happy?
- In spite of this God looked after Joseph.
- When we do naughty things we make Mummy/Daddy/God sad.
- We have to say sorry to Mummy/Daddy/God.
- When we say sorry to God he forgives us.
- God looks after us, just like he did Joseph.

Prayer

Dear God, when we do naughty things we make you sad. Thank you for looking after Joseph, even though he did naughty things. Thank you for looking after us. Amen.

Visual aids

Pictures from a Child's Story Bible.

Activities

1. Photocopy page 19 for each child. The children colour Joseph and his special coat.

2. Photocopy page 20 for each child. The children colour the pictures and glue cotton wool balls onto the sheep.
   Talk about the shepherd caring for the sheep, even when they are naughty and run away. God cares for us like a shepherd cares for his sheep.

Jacob loved Joseph more than his other sons. He made him a special coat.

God looked after Joseph.

God cares for you.   1 Peter 5:7

Joseph Saves his Family

Lesson aim: to show that God provides for his people.

Preparation

1. Read Genesis 39:1 - 45:28.

2. Answer the following questions:
   - list the bad things that happened to Joseph.
   - how do we know that God was in control? (39:2,20-21; 41:25,39-40; 45:7)
   - list everything that happened to Joseph in these chapters. How did God prepare Joseph for his role as saviour of his people?

3. Think about the way God used circumstances to change Joseph. Can you think of any circumstances God has used to make you more Christ-like?

4. Pray for the children, asking God to help you teach them that they can trust him to provide for their needs. Give some thought to the practical ways God does this, e.g. through parents.

5. Choose appropriate visual aids.

In this lesson we are seeking to give the children an overview of the story. Their concentration span is too short to allow the inclusion of much of the detail.

Remind the children of last week's story - Joseph sold as a slave and taken to Egypt. Make sure they realise what a slave did.

When Joseph arrived in Egypt he was bought by the Captain of the Guard. God was with Joseph and so everything Joseph did turned out well. Joseph was put in charge of the Captain's house.

The Captain's wife told lies about Joseph so he was put in prison. But God was with Joseph and so everything that Joseph did turned out well. Joseph was put in charge of the prisoners.

Some time later two of the king's servants were put in prison. One night they both had a dream. Because God was with Joseph he knew what the dreams meant. Joseph told the king's servants the meaning of their dreams. What Joseph said came true.

Two years later the king had a dream. When he woke up he asked all his wise men to tell him the meaning of the dream. But none of knew. Then his servant remembered that Joseph knew what dreams meant. The servant told the king about Joseph.

The king sent for Joseph from prison and told him his dream. Because God was with Joseph he could tell the king what his dream meant.

This is the meaning of the dream. There was going to be a famine. (Explain a famine.) For 7 years there would be plenty of food. Then, for 7 years there would be no food. The king asked Joseph what they should do, and Joseph told him. Then the king put Joseph in charge. Everyone in the land of Egypt had to do what Joseph said.

When the famine came, Jacob (Joseph's father) and Joseph's brothers ran out of food. They were very hungry. They came to Egypt to buy food. Joseph was very pleased to see them again and asked them all to come to Egypt to live. So all of Jacob's family had food to eat, because God was with Joseph.

Recap on the ways God looked after Joseph and his family.

Prayer

Dear God, thank you for looking after Joseph and his family. Thank you for looking after us. Amen.

Visual aids

Pictures from a Child's Story Bible.

Activities

1. Act out the story. Direct the children for each scene.

2. Give each child a sheet of paper with the following verse written on the bottom, *God will meet all your needs. Philippians 4:19.* Provide cut-outs from magazines of food, clothes, toys, etc. Ask the children what their needs are, and as each one is mentioned get the children to pick out appropriate cut-outs and stick them on to their paper. Talk about the way God provides for us.

Moses in the Reeds

Lesson aim: to teach that God is able to protect.

Preparation

1. Read Exodus 1:8 - 2:10.

2. Answer the following questions:
   - why did Pharaoh make the Israelites slaves?
   - why did Pharaoh order the boys to be killed and not the girls?
   - how did God protect Moses?

3. Last week we saw how God saved his people from starvation. Now they are in an even worse state - slaves in Egypt. Think about God's sovereignty - nothing happens outside his control. God took his people to Egypt. Over the next 3 lessons we will see how God rescues his people and takes them back to the Promised Land.

4. Thank God that he is a rescuing God. Ask him to help you teach the children about his loving care for them.

5. Prepare visual aids.

Remind the children of the things they have been learning about God - he looks after them (lesson 7), he keeps his promises (lesson 5), he wants them to be his friends (lesson 4). Remind them that God looks after them. Today we are going to find out how God looked after a tiny baby.

Tell the story from Moses' mother's point of view. *(See visual aids section for what is needed.)*

Remind the children that they heard about Joseph last week, and his father and brothers coming to live in Egypt.

A long time after Joseph died there was a new king in Egypt. He didn't know about Joseph. Joseph's family were called Israelites There were so many of them that the king was frightened of them. So he made them his slaves. They had to do what he told

them. He made them build big cities and it was very hard work.

The Israelites had lots of babies, so the king ordered all the boy babies to be killed. Then they couldn't grow up and fight against him. I had a little boy and his name was Moses. *(Take out doll.)*

When he was born I hid him away, but soon he got too big and noisy and I couldn't hide him anymore. I didn't want him to be killed, so I put him into a basket that would float. *(Put the doll in a basket.)*

I placed the basket in the river near the edge. *(Place basket on blue cloth on table.)* I told my daughter to hide and watch what happened to Moses.

The king's daughter came to wash in the river. She heard Moses crying. When she saw him she wanted him to be her own son. My daughter, Miriam, asked the princess if she would like someone to look after the baby. The princess said yes, so Miriam ran to fetch me. The princess asked me to look after Moses for her. (Take the doll out of basket).

When Moses was old enough I took him to the king's daughter and now he lives with her. So God looked after Moses and kept him safe.

Prayer
Dear God, thank you for keeping Moses safe. Thank you for keeping us safe too. Amen.

Visual aids
A doll, a basket (a shoe box would do), a piece of blue cloth to be the river.

Activities
1. Use the template on page 23 to cut one Moses' basket per child from card (e.g. cereal packets). Colour appropriately and write on each, *God kept Moses safe*. Provide grass or leaves for each child to glue onto the basket as reeds.

2. Cover the template on page 23 with a piece of plain paper, then photocopy pages 23 and 24 back to back for each child. Cut along the edges of the reeds at the bottom of page 23. Fold up along the dotted line to see reeds and sky. When the page is unfolded Moses can be seen safe in his basket. The children colour page 24 and the reeds on page 23.

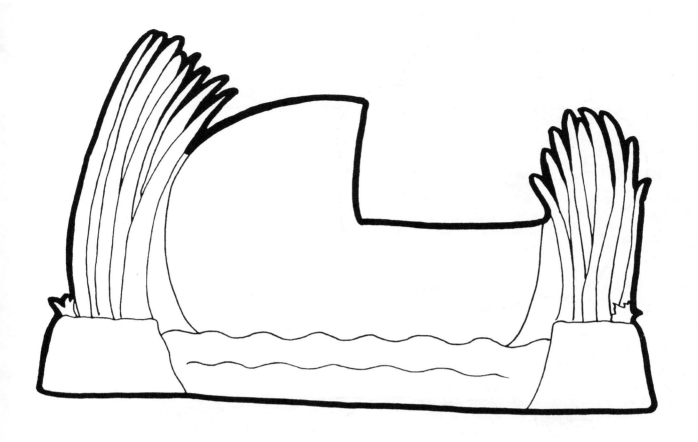

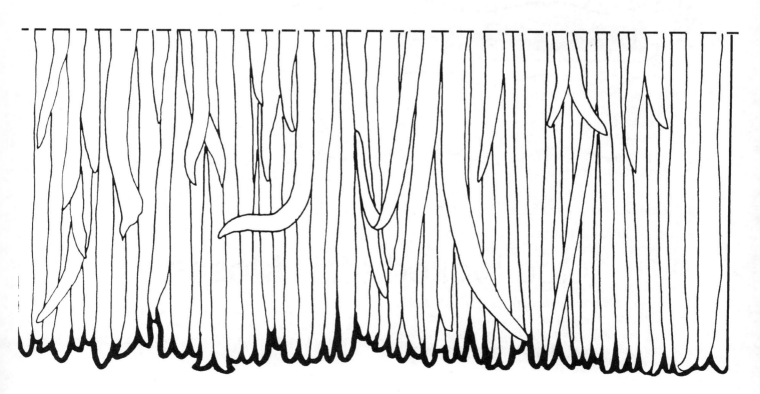

God looked after Moses.

Moses at the Burning Bush

> **Lesson aim:** to show how God provided help for his people.

Preparation

1. Read Exodus 2:23 - 4:31.

2. Answer the following questions:
   - did God know what was happening to his people? (2:23-25)
   - what was Moses doing when God spoke to him? (3:1-2)
   - what job did God give Moses? (3:7-10)
   - what 5 excuses did Moses make and how did God answer them? (3:11-15; 4:1-17)
   - what did God tell Moses about the difficulties he would face? (3:18-20; 4:21-23)
   - how did the elders respond to what Moses told them? (4:29-31)

3. God's name signified God's character. Think about the significance of God calling himself the God of Abraham, Isaac and Jacob. What understanding of God's character does this give?

4. Pray for the children you teach, asking God to open their eyes to who he is.

5. Choose appropriate visual aids.

Remind the children of last week's lesson - Moses the baby saved from death and brought up in the king's palace. God had a special job for Moses. Today we will find out what the job was.

After Moses grew up he left the king's palace and went to live in another country. He became a shepherd and looked after sheep. One day Moses was looking after his sheep when he saw something very strange. A bush was on fire but it wasn't burning up. Moses went closer to see why this was.

As Moses came closer God called out to him from the bush, *'Moses, Moses.'*

God told Moses not to come any closer. God told him to take his shoes off, because he was standing on holy ground. (Explain to the children that people in Eastern countries still do this today when they go to their holy places.) Moses did as God told him.

Then God told Moses that he knew his people were very sad. He knew how hard it was for them to be slaves in Egypt. God told Moses to go back to Egypt to rescue his people and take them back to the special land God had given them.

God told Moses he would give him special powers so that the people would believe that God had sent him. *(Tell the children about the stick turning into a snake.)*

Moses was very worried about going back to Egypt. He didn't think he was good enough to do the job God told him to do. So God said he would give Moses his brother Aaron as a helper.

Moses did what God said - he went back to Egypt and told God's people that God was going to rescue them. Then Moses went with his brother Aaron to see the king, to ask him to let the Israelite slaves go.

Prayer
Dear God, thank you that you hear your people when they pray to you. Thank you for helping us when we need it. Amen.

Visual aids
Pictures from a Child's Story Bible.

Activities
1. Photocopy page 26 for each child. Cut out red flames from gummed paper for the children to stick onto the bush (see diagram). The page can be coloured.

2. Make a headband. Photocopy page 27 on card for each child. Cut out the 2 pieces and staple or sellotape together at one end. The children colour the headbands. The sheep can be decorated by having cotton wool balls glued on their bodies.

God spoke to Moses from the burning bush.

The Lord said, "I have seen the misery of my people in Egypt. ..... I have come down to rescue them."

Exodus 3:7-8

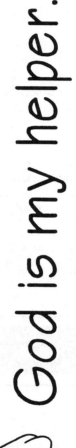

God is my helper.

God Saves his People

> **Lesson aim:** to teach that God is all powerful, by showing how he saved his people from the Egyptians.

Preparation

1. Read Exodus 14:1-31.

2. Answer the following questions:
   - why did the Israelites camp by the sea? (v.1-3)
   - why did the Egyptians chase after the Israelites? (v.5-9)
   - how did the Israelites react when they saw the approaching Egyptians? (v.10-12)
   - how did God save his people?
   - what was the result? (v.4,31)

3. The Israelites quickly lost faith in God's power to save them. Think about God's power and how you can teach the children that God can do anything - even the miraculous.

4. Pray for the children you teach, that they may learn that God can do anything.

5. Choose and prepare appropriate visual aids.

Remind the children of the lessons about Moses. If the lessons on the plagues and Passover have not been covered (OT1 and OT2), the following summary should be used.

When Moses and Aaron asked the king to let God's people go the king said, 'No!' So God made lots of bad things happen in Egypt. *(Tell the children about a couple of the plagues.)* Each time something bad happened the king promised to let God's people go. As soon as God took away the *(frogs, hail, etc.)* the king changed his mind and refused to let the people go. Then God said that all the Egyptians' oldest sons would die on the same night, but all the Israelites' sons would be safe. Everything happened just like God said. Then the king told Moses to take God's people and leave Egypt.

Moses led God's people away from Egypt. They got as far as the Red Sea. But there they were stuck - and the Egyptians were coming after them!

When the people saw the Egyptians they were very afraid. They started to complain to Moses. Moses told them to trust God and he would save them. Then God told Moses to stretch out his rod over the sea. Moses did what God said. God made the sea stand up and all the people walked over on dry land. The Egyptians didn't love God. They began to chase God's people into the sea - but God closed it over them. All the Israelites thanked God for saving them, as only he could.

Stress lesson aim at this point.

Prayer

Dear God, thank you that you can do anything. Amen.

Visual aids

Either pictures from a Child's Story Bible or the following.

Requirements:
- roll of blue paper (paper must be of the type that will roll back if unrolled and let go suddenly).
- photocopy the Egyptians on page 29, and the Israelites on page 30. Cut out the Israelites and the Egyptians, colour and glue onto card so that they will stand up.

Procedure:
1. Cut a length of blue paper to form a river. Roll up the remaining paper from both ends so they meet in the middle. Paint a section in the middle to look like the sea bed.
2. Prior to the lesson attach the river to a firm base, e.g. a table top. Attach the roll of paper to river so that 'sea bed' is firmly anchored. Let the paper roll together in the centre.
3. During the story bring the crowd of Israelites to the edge of river. At the appropriate point unroll the paper and anchor both ends with bluetak or drawing pins. The Israelites can walk across the river bed, chased by Egyptian soldiers. When the Israelites are safe on the other side of the river, but the Egyptians are still in the middle, release both ends of the paper roll, which should then spring together, swallowing up the Egyptians.

Activities

1. Photocopy page 30 for each child. The children colour in the crowd. Each child needs 2 waves cut from one A4 sheet of blue paper (see diagram). Fasten the waves to the picture at X with a split pin paper fastener. Start with the waves shut, then open to show the Israelites walking across in safety.

2. Teach the following song to the tune of *'The wheels of the bus go round and round'*.

   **Moses and the people came to the sea,
   came to the sea, came to the sea.
   Moses and the people came to the sea,
   but they could not get across.**

   **God sent a wind to blow back the sea,
   blow back the sea, blow back the sea.
   God sent a wind to blow back the sea
   and the people walked across.**

   The following actions accompany the words:
   Moses and the people came to the sea - walk fingers.
   But they could not get across - shake head.
   God sent a wind to blow back the sea - move hands away from each other.
   And the people walked across - walk fingers.

The people cried to God for help.

God took them through the sea to safety. (Exodus 14:1-31)

x

God Provides for his People

Lesson aim: to show how God provided for his people's daily needs of food and guidance.

Preparation

1. Read Exodus 13:17-22; 16:1-30.

2. Answer the following questions:
   - why did God provide a physical symbol of his presence to guide the Israelites? (13:20-22)
   - Why did the Israelites grumble? (16:2-3)
   - What did the grumbling demonstrate about their relationship with God? (16:6-8)
   - Why did some of the people disobey Moses? (16:20,27)

3. Think about the way God had demonstrated his power both in Egypt and since leaving. It was only 2 months later (16:1) and the people seemed to have forgotten. Think about our need for constant reminders about God's character and power.

4. Pray for the children you teach, asking God to open their eyes to his loving care for them.

5. Choose and prepare appropriate visual aids.

Remind the children of the previous lessons about Moses. Talk about the ways God had looked after his people so far.

After God had brought his people out of Egypt, he led them towards the land he had promised to give to Abraham.

The people did not know the way, so God had to show them where to go. *(Discuss with the children how they know the way to go to places, e.g. Mummy or Daddy takes them.)*

Because we cannot see God, he could not just walk in front of his people to show them the way. So God provided a big pillar of cloud to go before them during the day, and a pillar of fire at night. Everywhere the pillar of cloud or fire went, the people followed, and when the pillar stopped, they stopped too.

The pillars of cloud and fire led the people through the desert. After they had been in the desert for many days the people started to grumble. They were hungry and there was nothing to eat. Instead of asking God for help, they grumbled to each other. They even started to wish they were back in Egypt!

God heard their grumbling and God sent special bread called 'manna'. The people found it on the ground outside their tents each morning when they woke up. And every evening God sent birds called quails for the people to catch and eat. During all the years that the Israelites were in the desert God never let them down. He gave them food every day, and showed them the right way to go.

Prayer

Dear God, thank you that you look after your people. Thank you for giving us our food today. Amen.

Visual aids

Photocopy page 32 twice. Cut out the 2 crowds and colour. Glue one crowd onto a sheet of paper with a desert scene and sun, and one onto a sheet of dark paper with a moon and stars. Make a pillar of cloud from cotton wool and a pillar of fire from red gummed paper. Stick the pillars onto the appropriate backgrounds with bluetak as the lesson progresses. Use pictures from a Child's Story Bible for the rest of the story. You can use Kellog's Frosties to illustrate manna (16:14,31).

Activities

1. Each child requires page 32 photocopied, one sun cut from yellow gummed paper and one pillar of cloud made from cotton wool balls. The children colour the crowd, then glue on the sun and pillar of cloud.

2. The children can make quails and manna from playdough (see the recipe in the visual aids section, page 79.)

3. Make a flag. Photocopy page 33 for each child. The children colour the picture, then glue the left side of the picture around a garden stick or length of dowel.

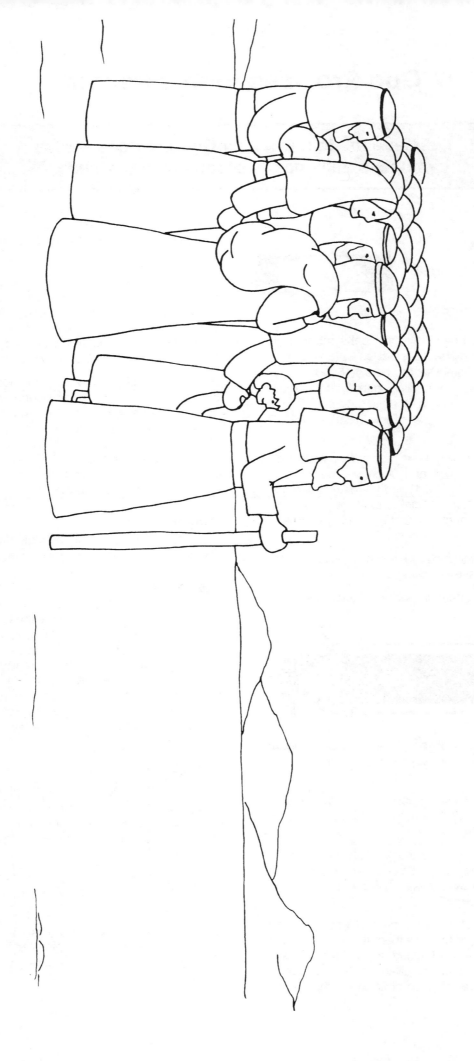

The Lord went ahead of them in a pillar of cloud to guide them on their way.   Exodus 13:21

God gave his people food to eat. (Exodus 16:1-30)

Lesson 12

Rahab Saves the Spies

> **Lesson aim: to show how God prepared the way for his people.**

Preparation

1. Read Joshua 2:1-24.

2. Answer the following questions:
   - why did Joshua send the spies? (v.1; 1:1-5)
   - why did Rahab hide them? (v.8-13)
   - was it right for Rahab to lie? (v.3-6 cf. Leviticus 19:11, Hebrews 11:31, James 2:25)
   - what did Rahab know about God?
   - cf. v.17-19 with Exodus 12:21-23. What similarities are present?

3. Rahab believed God's people would be victorious because of what she had heard. Think about the way you teach the children about God. Is the knowledge they are gaining helping them to put their trust in him?

4. Pray for the children you teach, asking God to open their eyes to who he is.

5. Choose appropriate visual aids.

Remind the children of the previous lessons about Moses. Talk about the way God led his people out of Egypt and provided for their needs in the wilderness.

Many years passed. All that time God's people wandered around in the desert. God gave them food to eat and water to drink. At last they came to the land that God promised to give them. But lots of other people lived in this land. They lived in towns with high walls around them. These people didn't want the Israelites (God's people) to come and live there. What should God's people do?

Moses had died and the Israelites had a new leader. His name was Joshua. He reminded the Israelites that God had promised to be with them. Did God keep his promises to Abraham? Did God keep his promises to Moses? So will God keep his promise to Joshua? Joshua said, *'God has promised to give us this land, so there is no need to be frightened.'*

There was a town called Jericho. It had very high walls. The Israelites had to capture Jericho before they could go into the rest of the land God had promised to give them. Joshua sent 2 men to Jericho to see if it was possible to capture it.

When the 2 men got to Jericho they went to Rahab's house. Rahab lived in a house on the town wall. Rahab had heard how God had brought his people out of Egypt. She believed that God would help them capture Jericho. She told the 2 spies how frightened the people in Jericho were.

The king of Jericho heard that the 2 spies were there. He sent soldiers to Rahab's house to arrest them. But Rahab hid the spies and told the soldiers that they had already left the town. So the soldiers went after the spies to catch them.

Rahab made the spies promise to save her and all her family when the Israelites captured Jericho. The spies told her to tie a piece of red cord to her window so that they would know which house to protect. If Rahab and her family stayed inside the house with the red cord at the window they would be safe. Then Rahab let the spies down the outside of the wall on a rope and they got away safely.

Prayer
Dear God, thank you that you always keep your promises. Thank you for your promise that you will never leave us. Amen.

Visual aids
Either pictures from a Child's Story Bible or models.

For models use a town wall made from cereal packets (see diagrams), 5 peg people - Rahab, 2 spies, 2 soldiers (see page 78), a rope to let the spies down the wall and a small piece of red wool with bluetak to attach it to the window.

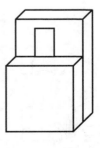

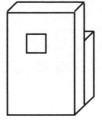

Activities

1. Photocopy page 35 for each child. Cut off the picture section. Cut out the spy from the top of the page. Using a needle and approximately 25 cm. of thread, attach the spy to the picture, starting at the **back**. Push the needle through X at the bottom man's hands, then through the spy's lower hand from the back at X, through X at the spy's upper hand, followed by X at Rahab's hands. Tie the thread at the back of the picture. The spy should move freely up and down the wall. The children colour the picture and glue a small piece of red wool to Rahab's window.

2. Play hunt the spies. One leader is Rahab and the other leader(s) is a soldier. The children are spies. The soldier(s) shuts eyes whilst Rahab hides the spies. The soldier(s) has to find the spies and catch them by tagging them. Once a spy is tagged he/she has to go to a designated area of the room and stay there until freed by Rahab. At the end ask the children, *'Why did Rahab keep the spies safe?'* The answer is because she believed God.

Rahab saved the spies because she believed what she had heard about God.

The Lord your God is God in heaven above and on the earth below.

Joshua 2:11

Lesson 13

The Battle of Jericho

> **Lesson aim: to teach that God can do the impossible.**

Preparation

1. Read Joshua 6:1-27.

2. Answer the following questions:
   - did God's instructions make sense in regard to the capture of Jericho? (v.2-5)
   - so why did the people do what Joshua said? (1:16-18; 3:7-17)
   - how many times in total did the Israelites march around Jericho? (v.3,-4)
   - on which circuit(s) of the city did the people shout and on which did they keep silent? (v.10,12-16)
   - why was Rahab and her family spared? (v.22-25) Rahab became one of Jesus' ancestors (Matthew 1:1-6).

3. Think about the way God demonstrated to his people that he could do the impossible. How does this passage help us to trust God in difficult times and situations?

4. Pray for the children, asking God to help you teach them accurately from his word.

5. Prepare visual aids.

Remind the children of the previous lesson on Joshua. After the 2 spies got back to the Israelite camp they told Joshua what they had found out in Jericho. *'Everyone is afraid of us,'* they said. *'Surely God will help us win.'* Off they went to Jericho.

When they got close by, God told Joshua what the people were to do. Before we hear what God said we all need to make trumpets. (See activity for instructions).

Get the children to help make Jericho (see visual aids). Explain to the children that they are the Israelites and the teacher is Joshua. The Israelites are to do what Joshua says.

Mark out an area for the Israelite's camp. Tell the children to march around Jericho blowing their trumpets, but not to shout. Then march them back to the camp. Repeat this 5 more times, explaining that it is performed once a day.

On the 7th day ask them to march around Jericho 7 times and on the 7th time to give a big shout.

The teacher stands in the middle of Jericho and, when the children shout, knocks the walls down flat. Then sit with the children and continue the story.

Do your remember what the spies promised Rahab? (If no answer is forthcoming, remind the children that Rahab and her family were to be saved). Joshua sent the 2 spies to save Rahab and all her family. Then the whole of Jericho was destroyed.

Stress the lesson aim at this point.

Prayer

Dear God, thank you that you always do what you say you will. Thank you that you can do what no one else can. Amen.

Visual aids

Use cushions or cardboard boxes to make Jericho.

Activities

1. Trumpets
   Use coloured cartridge paper or light card.
   Cut a 1/4 circle (see diagram). Write along the curved edge *The Lord your God will be with you wherever you go. Joshua 1:9.*
   The children decorate the trumpet. Fold into a trumpet shape and glue. Staple both ends.

2. Make a story box.
   Photocopy page 37 on card and page 38 on paper for each child. Make up the boxes following the instructions on page 37. Cut out the 4 pictures from page 38 and place in an envelope for each child.
   The children colour the pictures and glue them in order around the box.
   Use the story box to revise the story.

side 4

1. Cut out, score and fold along dotted lines.

2. Glue side 4 to the remaining 3 sides.

3. Glue the top flaps inside the sides to make a box open at the bottom.

God said to Joshua,

"I have delivered Jericho into your hands."

Joshua 6:2

God told Joshua what the people must do to capture Jericho.

Every day for 6 days, the people marched once round Jericho blowing their trumpets.

On the 7th day the people marched around Jericho 7 times, blowing their trumpets.

Then they gave a great shout and the walls of Jericho fell down, just as God said would happen.

Gideon

> **Lesson aim:** to teach that God saves his people from their enemies.

Preparation

1. Read Judges 7:1-23.

2. Answer the following questions:
   - why was Gideon also called Jerub-Baal? (6:27-32)
   - how big was the army Gideon summoned? (6:34-35; 7:3)
   - why did God say the army was too big? (v.2)
   - how did God whittle down the army to the right size? (v.3,5)
   - how big was the army God used to defeat the Midianites? (v.7)
   - how big was the Midianite army? (v.12; 8:10)
   - how did God give Gideon courage to attack? (v.9-15)
   - how were the Midianites defeated? (v.19-22)

3. Small children love battles. Think about how you can teach this story accurately, getting over the fact that it was God who won the battle, not the army.

4. Pray for each child you teach, asking God to open their eyes to his saving power.

5. Choose appropriate visual aids.

Start by seeing what they can remember of last week's lesson.

After God's people, the Israelites, came to the land God had promised would be theirs, they had many different leaders. One of these leaders was called Gideon. God used Gideon to save his people from their enemies.

Gideon collected all the men into a big army. It wasn't as big as the enemy army. But God told Gideon that the army was too big. When the Israelites won they would say that they had done it themselves because they were so many. So Gideon told the army that all the men who were afraid could go home. A lot did.

God said that the army was still too big. He told Gideon to take them to the river and let them drink. Most of the men knelt down to drink straight from the river. A few scooped up the water in their hands and drank. God told Gideon to take the 300 men who drank from their hands, and send the rest home.

That night God told Gideon to go down to the enemy camp and listen to what they were saying. Gideon went down and listened outside a tent. He heard the enemy soldiers say that God would give Gideon the victory over his enemies.

Gideon went back to his camp. He gave each of his soldiers a torch inside a jar and a trumpet. They surrounded the enemy's camp. The Israelites all blew on their trumpets and broke the jars so that the light shone from the torches. They all cried: *'For the Lord and for Gideon'*. The enemy soldiers were so frightened that they ran away.

That is how God saved his people, the Israelites, from their enemies.

Prayer

Dear God, thank you that you are a God who saves people. Amen.

Visual aids

Pictures from a Child's Story Bible.
Use the picture on page 40 to show what happened when the jars were broken.

Activities

1. Make a flaming torch. Cut one from yellow cartridge paper or light card for each child (see diagram). Write the verse on the handle, *I will deliver you. Judges 7:7.* Cut out flames from red and orange paper and place in an envelope for each child. The children glue red and orange flames onto the torch.

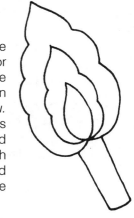

2. Photocopy page 40 for each child. Follow the instructions on page 40.

Gideon's army broke the pitchers and sounded the trumpets.

X

God said,
'I will deliver you.'
Judges 7:7

1. Cut off the bottom section of this page and cut out the circle.

2. Cut out the pitcher shape at the top of the torch.

3. The children colour half of the circle brown for the pitcher and half yellow/red for the torch.

4. Attach the circle behind the picture using a split pin paper fastener at X. The circle can be rotated to show what happened when the pitcher was broken.

5. The children colour the picture.

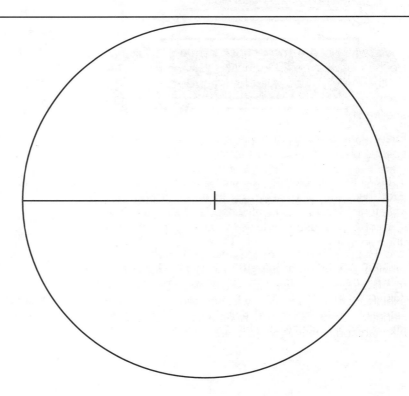

Hannah's Baby

Lesson aim: to teach that God hears our prayers.

Preparation

1. Read 1 Samuel 1:1-28.

2. Answer the following questions:
   - why was Hannah unhappy? (v.2-7)
   - what did Hannah do about her situation? (v.9-11)
   - what did Eli think was wrong with Hannah? (v.12-14)
   - what did Hannah promise to do if God answered her prayer? (v.11)
   - did Hannah keep her promise? (v.24-28)

3. Think about the comfort of knowing that God hears us when we pray. How does this knowledge affect the way we pray?

4. Thank God for the children you teach. Ask him to help you encourage the children to pray.

5. Choose and prepare visual aids.

There was once a man whose name was Elkanah. He had a wife called Hannah. Elkanah also had another wife. This wife had some children, but Hannah had none. Hannah was very sad because she wanted a baby.

Every year Elkanah and his family went to a very special church called the temple. Whilst they were there Hannah went to a part of the temple where she thought no one would see her and she prayed to God. She asked God to give her a son. Then she said that if God answered her prayer she would give her son back to God.

The High Priest was called Eli. He saw Hannah praying and thought that she had been drinking too much wine, so he went to scold her. But Hannah explained to Eli why she was so sad. Eli said to Hannah, *'May God do what you have asked.'* Elkanah and his family went home.

God heard Hannah's prayer and before the end of the year she had a baby boy. She called him Samuel.

When Samuel was old enough to leave his mother, Hannah took him to Eli, the High Priest, so that he could live and work in the temple. God had answered Hannah's prayer, and Hannah kept her promise to God.

Prayer

Dear God, thank you that you hear us when we pray. Amen.

Visual aids

Either pictures from a Child's Story Bible or models.

If using models you need yoghurt pot people (see page 78), an altar, a candlestick, and a temple made from a cardboard box with pillars made from paper towel centres.

The altar is made from a small box (matchbox) covered with gold paper.

The candlestick is cut out of gold card (see diagram). Glue a toothpick to the back of the upright with the point protruding from the base. The candlestick can be stuck into a blob of bluetak to make it stand up.

Activities

1. Each child requires a photocopy of page 42, and a sheet of A4 paper with *'I prayed for this child, and the Lord has granted me what I asked of him.'* 1 Samuel 1:27 written on the bottom. Cut out the 3 figures from page 42 and place in an envelope for each child. The children colour the figures of Hannah, Samuel and Eli and glue them onto the plain sheet to make up the picture of Samuel being taken to the temple

2. Make a baby in a cradle. Photocopy page 43 on card for each child. Prior to the lesson cut out the cradle and the baby. Score and fold along the dotted lines of the cradle.
The children colour the cradle and the baby. Help them to fold the cradle along the dotted lines and glue the tabs to the inside. The baby is folded into a cone shape and glued. Place the baby in the cradle and cover with a scrap of material.

3. Encourage the children to pray, using short sentences. Talk about what they should pray for beforehand.

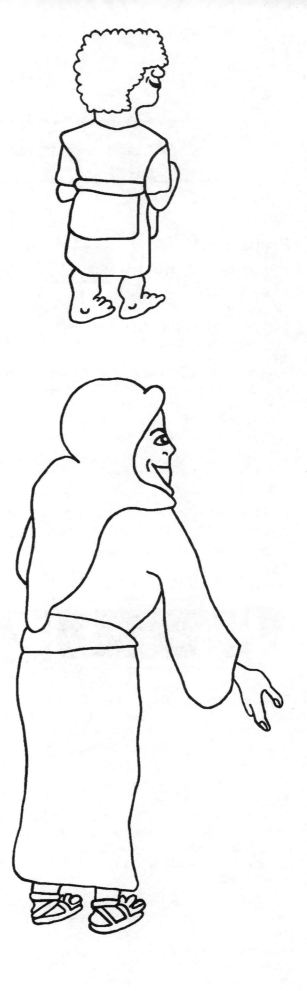

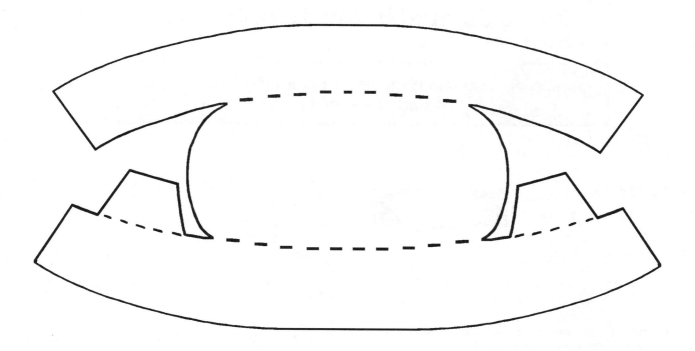

Samuel in the Temple

Lesson aim: to teach the importance of listening to God and obeying him.

Preparation

1. Read 1 Samuel 2:18-26; 3:1-21.

2. Answer the following questions:
   - what do we learn about Samuel from 2:18-26?
   - what do we learn about religious life at the time? (2:22-25; 3:1)
   - did Samuel have a relationship with God before God spoke to him? (2:18,21,26; 3:7)
   - what do we learn about Samuel's obedience? (3:4-18)
   - did Eli accept God's sovereignty? (3:18)

3. Samuel was taught obedience from an early age. Think about how you can lovingly encourage the children in your care to develop this quality.

4. Pray for the children, asking God to give them hearts that want to obey him.

5. Prepare visual aids.

Remind the children of last week's story about the birth of Samuel.

Samuel lived with Eli, the High Priest, in the temple. Eli taught Samuel how to serve God.

Eli had 2 sons. They were also priests. Eli was very old and his 2 sons were very naughty. They disobeyed God. They would not listen to Eli when he told them to stop disobeying God. But Samuel listened to Eli and did the things that pleased God.

One night, when Eli and Samuel were both in bed, God called to Samuel, saying, 'Samuel, Samuel.'

Samuel thought it was Eli calling, and went to him. Eli sent him back to bed. This happened 3 times. At last Eli realised that it was God who was calling Samuel. He told Samuel to go back to bed and when God called again to say, 'Speak, Lord, your servant is listening.'

So Samuel went back to bed, and God called to him again. 'Samuel, Samuel.' Samuel did as Eli told him. He said, 'Speak, your servant is listening.' God told Samuel that he was going to punish Eli's sons for their wickedness and they would not be priests when Eli died.

But Samuel grew up to do the things that pleased God. God chose Samuel to be his priest and to tell his people what they should do.

Prayer

Dear God, help us to listen to your word and to do what it says. Amen.

Visual aids

As for the previous lesson. Add in a small pot person for Samuel as a boy (see page 78) and 2 beds and covers - 1 for Eli and 1 for Samuel.

Activities

1. Give each child a sheet of paper with *'Live as the Lord wants and always do what pleases him. Colossians 1:10'* written on the bottom.
   Discuss with the children how God speaks to us to-day from the Bible, and what things we do that please God, e.g. picking up our toys, coming when Mummy or Daddy calls, bringing something when asked. Provide cut outs for the children to stick onto their paper, e.g. picture of a Bible, child helping a parent, picking up toys, etc. (see page 45).

2. Make a bib for each child to go over their head with a front and back. Provide 2 roundels for each child to glue onto the front and back (see diagram). A rectangle of paper with the words *Super Sam* is glued underneath roundel at the front. Write on the front, *'Live as the Lord wants. Colossians 1:10'* and on the back, *'Speak, for your servant is listening. 1 Samuel 3:10'*

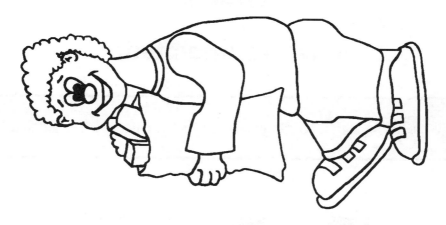

helping

putting toys away

going when Mummy
calls

David Anointed

Lesson aim: to show that God looks on the heart.

Preparation

1. Read 1 Samuel 16:1-13.

2. Answer the following questions:
   - why did Samuel think Eliab was God's chosen king? (v.6)
   - what does God say is the most important thing to consider? (v.7)

3. Think about how easy it is to be swayed by external appearances. Are there any children in your care that you find unattractive? How can you make sure you avoid favouritism?

4. Pray for the children you teach, asking God to help you treat them all alike.

5. Choose and prepare visual aids.

Remind the children of the previous 2 lessons about Samuel. By this time Samuel was an old man. He was God's special messenger to the Israelites (God's people). He told the people what God wanted them to do.

It was time to choose a new king in Israel and God told Samuel to go to see a man called Jesse. Jesse had 8 sons and God would show Samuel which one of them was to be the future king.

When Samuel arrived, Jesse lined up his 7 big sons. *'He must be this one,'* thought Samuel as he came to the first and the biggest son. *'No!'* said God, *'I haven't chosen him.'* *'He must be this one, then,'* thought Samuel as he came to the next one. *'No!'* said God again. *'Remember, I have chosen someone because he loves me most, not because he looks big and strong.'*

Samuel went down the line and each time God said, *'No!'* until there were no more sons left. *'Do you have any one else?'* Samuel asked Jesse. *'Well yes,'* said

Jesse, *'but he's very young. His name is David and he's looking after the sheep.'*

They fetched David and God said to Samuel, *'This is the one I have chosen, because he loves me.'* So Samuel anointed David to be the next king.

Prayer

Dear God, thank you that you know what we are really like. Please help us to love you with all our hearts. Amen.

Visual aids

Pictures from a Child's Story Bible or finger puppets.

For finger puppets you need Samuel, Jesse, 7 sons, and David (see page 79). Put Samuel on a finger of one hand and the others on the other hand, one at a time. Stand them on the table in a line as you finish with each one.

Activities

1. Make finger puppets of Samuel and David (see page 79). Make 1 set for each child. The puppets should be coloured by the children before they are glued.

2. Photocopy page 47 for each child. Cut the page in half along the dotted line. Cut around the solid line of the flap on David's chest and fold back along the dotted line. Glue the 2 halves of the page together at the sides, top and bottom with David on the outside. The flap on David's body can be opened to show his heart underneath.

God chose David to be the next king.

Man looks at the outward appearance,
but the Lord looks at the heart.
1 Samuel 16:7

Lesson 18

David Fights Goliath

Lesson aim: to teach that God helps those who trust him.

Preparation

1. Read 1 Samuel 17:1-58.

2. Answer the following questions:
   - look at the description of Goliath in v.4-7. Humanly speaking, did David have any chance of defeating him?
   - why did David go to the battle zone? (v.12-19)
   - why did David want to fight Goliath? (v.26,36,45)
   - why was David confident he could defeat Goliath? (v.34-37,46-47)

3. Consider what this passage teaches about trusting God to help in times of need. We need to remember that David's victory over Goliath was as the Lord's anointed (1 Samuel 16:12) and points to Christ. We are not in David's position.

4. Pray for the children, asking God that what you teach them week by week will help them to put their trust in him for salvation.

5. Choose appropriate visual aids.

Remind the children of last week's story about the anointing of David. Today we are going to hear about something that happened to David before he became king.

God's people were fighting against some people called the Philistines. These people didn't love God. Every morning they sent out a very big soldier called Goliath to stand before the Israelite army. He said that he would fight one of God's people to decide the battle. **All** the Israelites were afraid, even though God had promised to be with them. Every morning Goliath laughed at the Israelites because they were afraid.

One day David's father asked him to take some food to his 3 oldest brothers, who were soldiers in the army. David left his sheep in the care of another shepherd and did what his father asked. When he came to the Israelite camp he heard Goliath shouting his challenge as he did every morning. When David heard Goliath laughing at God's people, he was very angry. *'How dare someone say he could beat God's people,'* he said. *'I will fight him and God will help me.'*

When the king heard that David wanted to fight Goliath he was amazed. He told David he was too young. But David told the king how God had helped him kill lions and bears that tried to take his sheep. The king gave David his own armour to wear but it was much too big. So David took it off and went to meet Goliath just with his sling and 5 stones. (Explain a sling.)

Goliath laughed when he saw how little David was. *'You come to fight with lots of weapons,'* said David, *'but I come in God's name.'* Then David took his sling and 1 stone, and threw it at the big soldier. The stone hit him on the forehead and he fell down dead. Then all the Philistines ran away. God's people had won the battle, all because David trusted God.

Prayer
Dear God, please help us to trust you to look after us. Amen.

Visual aids
Pictures from a Child's Story Bible.

Activities
1. Make a cone figure of David. Photocopy page 49 on card for each child. Prior to the lesson cut out the appropriate pieces and place in an envelope for each child.
   The children colour the pieces. Help them fold the body into a cone shape and glue it together. Place the head on the body by placing the long tab through the hole at the top of the cone. Staple or glue the base of the tab to the inside of the body front. Glue the bag and sling at the edge of David's hands.

2. Photocopy page 50 for each child. The children colour the picture then glue a piece of material cut in the shape of a bag to David's right hand. Attach a rubber band to David's left hand for the sling using sellotape. Glue on 5 round pieces of grey paper beside David for the stones.

Cone People - David and Moses (see page 76)

Requirements

For David cut out the body, David's head, bag and sling.

For Moses cut out body, Moses' head and headdress.

Moses

David

The Lord will deliver me.   1 Samuel 17:37

Lesson 19

Solomon

> **Lesson aim:** to teach that God gives us what we need to do his work.

Preparation

1. Read 1 Kings 3:1-28.

2. Answer the following questions:
   - what was Solomon's relationship with God? (v.3-14)
   - why did Solomon ask God for wisdom? (v.7-9)
   - what did God promise to give him? (v.10-14)
   - what was the result of Solomon's ruling regarding the mother of the baby? (v.28)

3. Think about the way Solomon demonstrated wisdom in v.16-27. Think about how you can tell this story simply and accurately without dwelling on the baby being divided.

4. Pray for wisdom in your dealings with the children you teach.

5. Choose appropriate visual aids.

Lesson

Remind the children of the previous 2 lessons about David. Eventually David became king. He was king for many years. He was a very good king. He tried to do what God wanted and he made God very pleased. David grew old and died. His son, Solomon, became king.

King Solomon loved God. One night God appeared to him in a dream. God said, *'What would you like me to give you?'* Solomon said, *'Please make me wise so that I can look after your people properly. Help me know the difference between good and evil.'*

God was pleased that Solomon had asked for wisdom. God said, *'Because you have asked for wisdom and not for lots of money and a long life, I will do what you have asked. And I will give you lots of money and a long life as well.'*

One day 2 ladies came to see Solomon. They had 1 baby between them. Each lady said that the baby was hers. King Solomon had to decide who was the baby's real mother. King Solomon sent for a sword. When it came he said, *'Cut the baby in two and give half to each lady.'*

The real mother said, *'Please don't hurt the baby. Give it to the other lady.'* But the other lady said, *'Cut the baby in half.'* Then King Solomon knew who the real mother was. He said, *'Give the baby to the mother who didn't want the baby killed. She is the real mother.'*

When all the people heard what had happened they knew that God had given Solomon the wisdom to look after them properly.

Prayer

Dear God, please give us wisdom so that we know what the right thing is to do. Amen.

Visual aids

Pictures from a Child's Story Bible.

Activities

1. Make a crown. Cut out the 2 halves of the crown from an A4 sheet of card (see diagram). Cut off the 2 black triangles and discard.

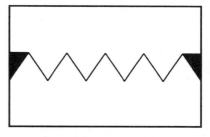

Write on one half, 'God gave Solomon wisdom to be a good king.' Staple the 2 halves together at one end. The children colour and decorate their crowns with coloured stars, pieces of silver foil, coloured paper shapes, etc. Fit the crown onto the child's head and staple/sellotape the 2 ends together.

2. Make a booklet. Photocopy pages 52/53 and 54/55 back to back for each child. Fold them in half and staple at the join to make an 8 page booklet. Go through the story with the children. The children can colour their booklets.

Wise King Solomon

1 Kings 3:1-28

God said to Solomon:

"I will give you a wise and discerning heart."

1 Kings 3:12

Solomon knew who was the real mother.

He gave the baby to her.

One night King Solomon had a dream.

In the dream God said, "Ask me for whatever you want and I will give it to you."

King Solomon said, "Cut the baby in half and give half to each mother."

The real mother said, "Don't kill the baby. Give him to the other lady."

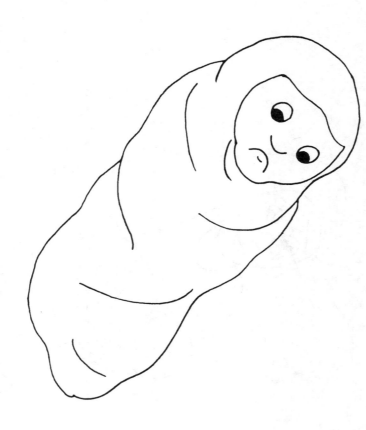

6

Solomon asked for wisdom so that he could be a good King over God's people.

3

Two ladies came to Solomon for help.

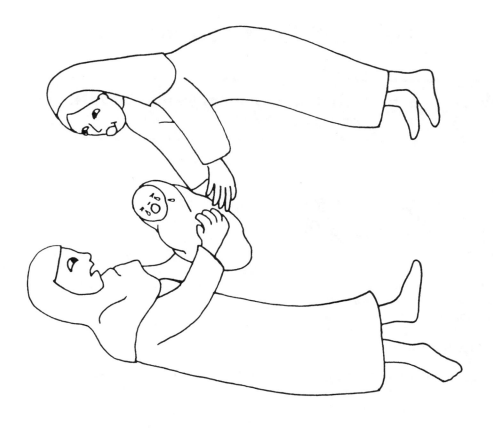

Each lady said, "This is my baby."

5

They had one baby between them.

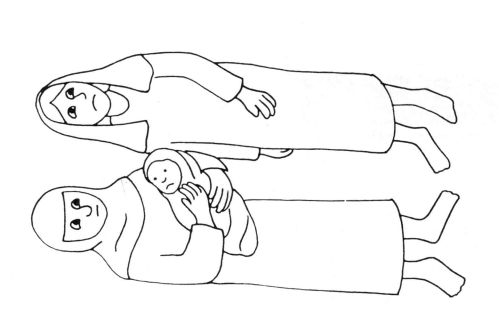

4

Lesson 20

Elijah and the Drought

> **Lesson aim: to teach that God supplies the needs of those who obey him.**

Preparation

1. Read 1 Kings 17:1-16.

2. Answer the following questions:
   - what sort of king was Ahab? (16:29-33)
   - Baal-melqart was a Phoenician god who was thought to control the weather. His worship was introduced into Israel by Ahab and his queen, Jezebel. What was God demonstrating in v.1?
   - what instructions did God give Elijah? (v.3-4,9)
   - Zarephath was in Phoenicia, Baal-melqart's territory. Did they have a drought there, as well as in Israel? (v.14)
   - how does this passage demonstrate that Elijah was a true prophet? (v.1,7,13-14.16)

3. Think about what this passage teaches about God. How does this knowledge help you in your everyday life?

4. Pray for the children, that they may learn more about God's faithfulness.

5. Choose appropriate visual aids.

Our story today is about a man called Elijah. Elijah was a prophet. God's prophets were people who brought messages from God about things that would happen in the future. When God's people were being naughty, God would send a prophet to tell them to stop or God would punish them. The people knew who were real prophets, because what they said would happen did happen.

Ask if anyone can remember the name of the wise king from last week's story.

After Solomon died there were other kings in Israel. One of these was called Ahab. He was very wicked and cruel and did not follow God. So God sent Elijah to Ahab with a message from God.

Elijah told Ahab that there would be no more rain for 3 years. (Discuss with the children what it would mean to have no rain). God told Elijah to go and hide in a special place near a brook so that he could have water to drink. Elijah did as God said. God sent ravens with food for Elijah every night and every morning.

At last the brook dried up, so God told Elijah to go to a certain town where a woman would feed him. Elijah did as God said.

When he arrived at the town he met a woman gathering a few sticks for a fire. Elijah asked the woman for a drink and some bread. She told him she only had enough food for one last meal for her and her son. Then her food jars would be empty. Elijah told her to make him a meal first and God would supply the food for her and her son. The woman did as Elijah said and made him a meal. Afterwards she found that she had plenty for her and her son also.

However much she used, her food jars remained full until the rains came again, just as God had promised.

Prayer
Dear God, please help us to be like Elijah and do what you say. Amen.

Visual aids
Pictures from a Child's Story Bible.

Activities
1. Act out the story with the children. Give directions for each scene as it occurs.

2. Photocopy page 57 for each child. Cut off the strip with the ravens and cut them out. The children colour the picture and glue on the ravens feeding Elijah.

God gave Elijah food and water.

The Lord alone is God.   1 Kings 18:39

Elisha and Naaman

> **Lesson aim:** to teach that God's grace is for all believers
> - Gentile as well as Jew.

Preparation

1. Read 2 Kings 5:1-16.

2. Answer the following questions:
   - was Naaman part of God's chosen people? (v.1, Genesis 12:1-3; 17:3-8)
   - was Naaman's condition serious? (v.6-7)
   - look at Naaman's reaction to Elisha's instructions (v.11-12). What was required from Naaman if he was to be cured? (v.13)
   - note how God dealt with Naaman's pride. Who told him what to do? (v.2-3,10,13)

3. In the time of Elisha Jews did not expect God's grace to be extended to the Gentile (outsider). Who do we class as outsiders? Are we guilty of denying them access to the grace of God?

4. Pray for the children you teach, that they may begin to understand that God's love is for everyone.

5. Choose appropriate visual aids.

Many, many years ago a man called Naaman lived in a country called Syria. He was Commander of the king's army. He didn't know about God.

One day Naaman noticed white patches on his skin. This was a disease called leprosy, which no one could make better. Naaman was very unhappy.

There was a little servant girl in Naaman's house who loved God. She told Naaman about God's special messenger called Elisha. Elisha was a prophet. (Ask the children if they can remember the name of the prophet in last week's story.) The servant girl told Naaman that God would help Elisha to make him better. So Naaman went to Israel, where God's people lived, to see Elisha.

Elisha told Naaman to go down to the river and jump in 7 times, and then he would be better. Naaman was cross at first because the river was dirty and there were much cleaner ones in Syria. He started to go home, but his servant persuaded him to do what Elisha said. So he went to the river and one, two, three, four, five, six times he jumped into the river and his skin looked exactly the same. But, after the seventh time, he came out completely cured. Naaman was so pleased. He thanked God straight away for making him better.

Prayer

Dear God, thank you that you love everyone and want everyone to follow you. Amen.

Visual aids

Either use pictures from a Child's Story Bible or models.

Models help demonstrate that the action took place in different locations. Use yoghurt pot people (see page 78). You require a serving girl, Naaman, Naaman's servant, Elisha and Elisha's servant. If you have sufficient space use 3 different tables - 1 for Naaman's house, 1 for Elisha's house and 1 for the river. Use a cardboard box with a door cut out of the front for Elisha's house. Use a strip of blue paper for the river and place it at the edge of the table next to the teacher. Naaman can be dipped in the teacher's lap.

Activities

1. Photocopy page 59 for each child. Cut off the strip at the top and cut out the figure of Naaman. Cut a slit in the river where marked. Fold the bottom of the page back along the dotted line and glue to the back of the picture along the sides to make a pocket. The children colour the river scene and Naaman. Naaman jumps in and out of the river through the slit.

2. Make a paper bag puppet for each child. Fold half an A4 sheet of paper in half and sellotape along the top and side to make a bag, open at the bottom. Draw a head without a mouth on each side. Make the face on 1 side blotchy. The children colour and draw a happy mouth on the cured side and an unhappy mouth on the blotchy side.

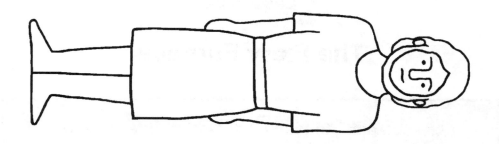

Elisha told Naaman to dip himself in the River Jordan 7 times.

Naaman did what Elisha said and God made him better.

(2 Kings 5:1-16)

The Fiery Furnace

Lesson aim: to teach that God is able to save.

Preparation

1. Read Daniel 3:1-30.

2. Answer the following questions:
   - the Babylonian empire was vast and incorporated people of many different nationalities. Why would it have been important for everyone to worship the same god? (v.1-6)
   - were the people told to stop worshipping their own God?
   - who did Nebuchadnezzar think was more powerful - him or God? (v.15)
   - did Shadrach, Meshach and Abednego's faith depend on their being saved from the furnace? (v.16-18)
   - was the furnace hot enough to kill the men? (v.22-23)
   - what was the result of the miracle? (v.28-30)

3. Think about the powerful God we serve and how difficult circumstances often help to confirm our faith.

4. Pray for the children you teach, that they may learn more about God's power to save.

5. Choose appropriate visual aids.

As time went by, God's people the Jews stopped following God. When they would not listen to him God allowed another people to capture them and take them away to another country called Babylon. Three young Jews were made governors in Babylon. Their names were Shadrach, Meshach and Abednego.

One day the king of Babylon made a huge statue out of gold. He said it was a god and ordered all the people in Babylon to worship it. If anyone refused to worship the statue they would be thrown into a very hot fire and burnt up. Shadrach, Meshach and Abednego were followers of God, so they refused to worship the statue.

The king was told that Shadrach, Meshach and Abednego refused to worship the statue. He sent for them and gave them one last chance to worship the statue or they would be thrown into the very hot fire and burnt up. The king told them that their God wouldn't be able to save them from the fire.

Shadrach, Meshach and Abednego knew that God can do anything. They knew God could save them from the fire. They said to the king, *'Our God is able to save us from the fire. But even if he chooses not to, we will not worship the statue.'* The king was very, very angry. He ordered the 3 men to be thrown into a hot, hot fire where they would be burnt up. The king did not believe that God could save them.

Shadrach, Meshach and Abednego were thrown into the fire, and what do you think happened? When the king looked at the fire he saw Shadrach, Meshach and Abednego walking in the fire unharmed. And someone else was with them who looked like the Son of God. The king called Shadrach, Meshach and Abednego to come out. They did so and none of them were harmed by the fire. Then the king praised God, because he had saved his followers from the fire.

Prayer
Dear God, thank you that you save your people. Amen.

Visual aids
Pictures from a Child's Story Bible.

Activities

1. Photocopy page 61 for each child. Cut the sheet in half and cut around the doors, so that they fold back on the dotted lines. Glue the 2 pieces together at top, bottom and sides so that the doors can be opened to show people in the furnace. The children colour the pictures.

2. Make a musical shaker. Each child requires a paper cup or toilet roll centre, rice/macaroni/dried peas, and a piece of colourful wrapping paper. Seal one end of the container. The children place the dried materials into the container, which is sealed with cling film. Glue a piece of wrapping paper round the container. Remind the children that the king praised God for saving the 3 men. Sing a simple praise song, using the shakers.

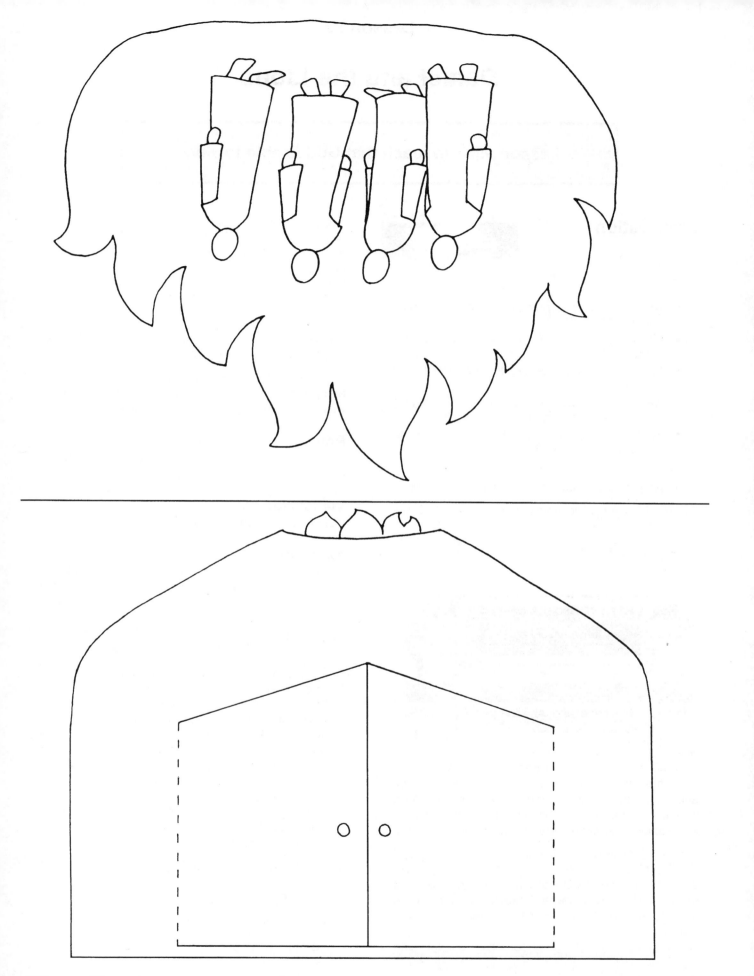

The God we serve is able to save us.   Daniel 3:17

Daniel and the Lions

Lesson aim: to teach that God is able to save.

Preparation

1. Read Daniel 6:1-28.

2. Answer the following questions:
   - what was Daniel's position in the government and why? (v.1-4)
   - note the 'all agreed' in v.7. Had Daniel agreed?
   - for how long were people to pray only to the king? (v.7)
   - was Daniel more ostentatious in his praying once the edict had been issued? (v.10)
   - what was the result of Daniel's refusal to compromise? (v.25-28)

3. Think about how easy it is to compromise in our worship of God. How can we guard against this?

4. Pray for each child you teach, that they will put their trust in God.

5. Choose appropriate visual aids.

Remind the children of last week's story about Shadrach, Meshach and Abednego saved by God from the fiery furnace.

Shadrach, Meshach and Abednego had a friend called Daniel. The king of Babylon made Daniel the chief governor. The other governors were jealous and set out to get rid of Daniel. They watched Daniel to see if he did anything wrong. But Daniel did his job properly - he wasn't lazy, he didn't cheat or lie.

The other governors knew that Daniel worshipped God, so they went to the king and asked him to make a law which said that no one was to pray to anyone except the king for 30 days. If they did they would be put into a den of lions. The king did as he was asked.

But Daniel could not obey this law. He continued to pray to God just as he had always done. Three times a day, Daniel knelt in front of his open window,

looking towards his own country, and prayed to God. The governors watched Daniel to see if he would break the new law. When they saw him praying to God, they went to the king and told him that Daniel had disobeyed the law. The king was very sad, because he liked Daniel, but he had to do what the law said.

So Daniel was thrown into the lion's den and it was sealed with a big stone. The king went away sad.

The next morning the king ordered the lion's den to be opened. And what do you think he found? Daniel was alive. God had saved him from the lions.

Prayer
Dear God, thank you that you save your people. Amen.

Visual aids
Pictures from a Child's Story Bible.

Activities
1. Photocopy page 63 for each child. Cut the sheet in half and cut around the doors, so that they fold back on the dotted lines. Glue the 2 pieces together at top, bottom and sides so that the doors can be opened to show Daniel unharmed by the lions. The children colour the pictures.

2. Make a lion mask. Each child requires page 64 photocopied on yellow card and half an A4 sheet of yellow paper. Prior to the lesson, cut out the mask and the eye holes. Attach a length of shearing elastic to both sides. Cut the yellow paper into strips approximately 1cm wide and 4cm long. Pull the strips through the blades of a pair of scissors to make them curl. Place the strips in an envelope for each child.
   The children glue the strips of yellow paper all the way round the face behind the head so that they curl out and make a mane.

3. Sing the praise song learnt last week.

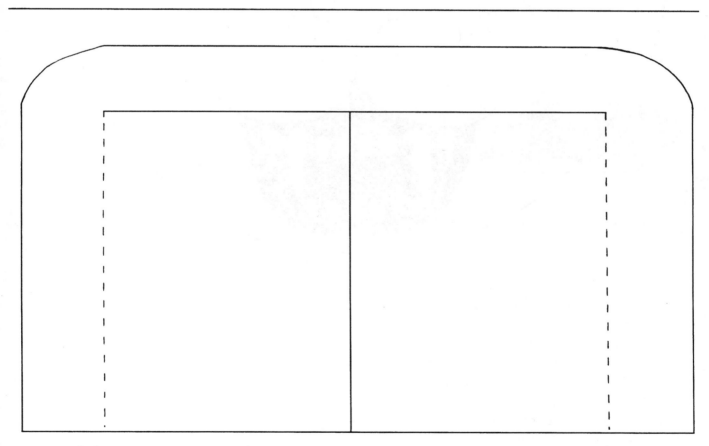

May your God, whom you serve continually, rescue you.   Daniel 6:16

Lion Mask

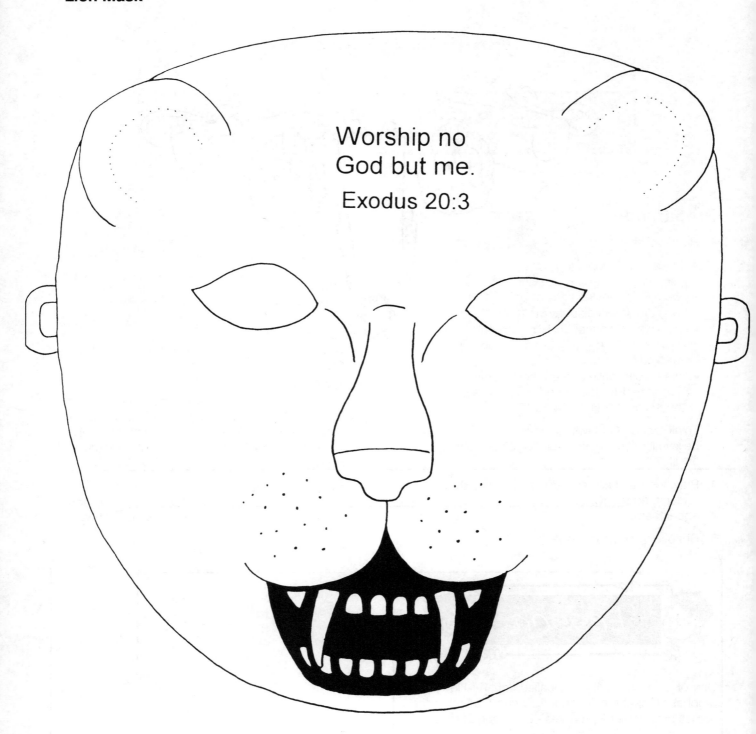

Worship no
God but me.
Exodus 20:3

Jonah Disobeys God

> **Lesson aim:** to teach that God is everywhere and we cannot get away from him.

Preparation

1. Read Jonah 1:1 - 2:10.

2. Answer the following questions:
   - were God's instructions clear? (1:1-2)
   - why did Jonah disobey? (1:3; 4:1-3)
   - who was in control - God or Jonah?
   - how did God get Jonah to do what God wanted?
   - what similarities are there between what happened to Jonah and Christ's saving death on the cross? (1:11,14-15,17)

3. Think about God's omnipresence. Do I really believe it? If so, how does this affect the way I live my life?

4. Pray for the children you teach, that they may understand that God is everywhere and knows all about them.

5. Choose appropriate visual aids.

One of God's servants was called Jonah. He was a prophet. (Ask the children if they can remember the names of the other 2 prophets - Elijah and Elisha.)

God told Jonah to go to a big city called Nineveh, where the people were very wicked, and tell them that God was going to punish them.

Jonah did not like the people in Nineveh, so he disobeyed God and caught a boat going in the opposite direction. Jonah tried to run away from God.

God sent a big storm and the boat was in danger of sinking. The sailors tried hard to get the boat to land, but could not. Jonah realised that it was all his fault and told the sailors to throw him overboard.

The sailors threw Jonah into the sea and the storm stopped. Jonah sank down into the water, but God sent a big fish to swallow Jonah and save him from drowning. Jonah thanked God for saving him.

After 3 days the fish spat Jonah out onto a beach.

Prayer

Dear God, please help us to do what you say. Amen.

Visual aids

Pictures from a Child's Story Bible.

Activities

1. Photocopy page 66 for each child. Cut out the big fish and Jonah The children colour Jonah and both sides of the fish. Glue the fish together at the tail and around the sides. Leave the mouth end open so that Jonah can be popped inside.

2. Play a hiding game. Hide with the children in different places, e.g. under the table, behind some chairs. Each time ask, *'Does God know where we are?'*

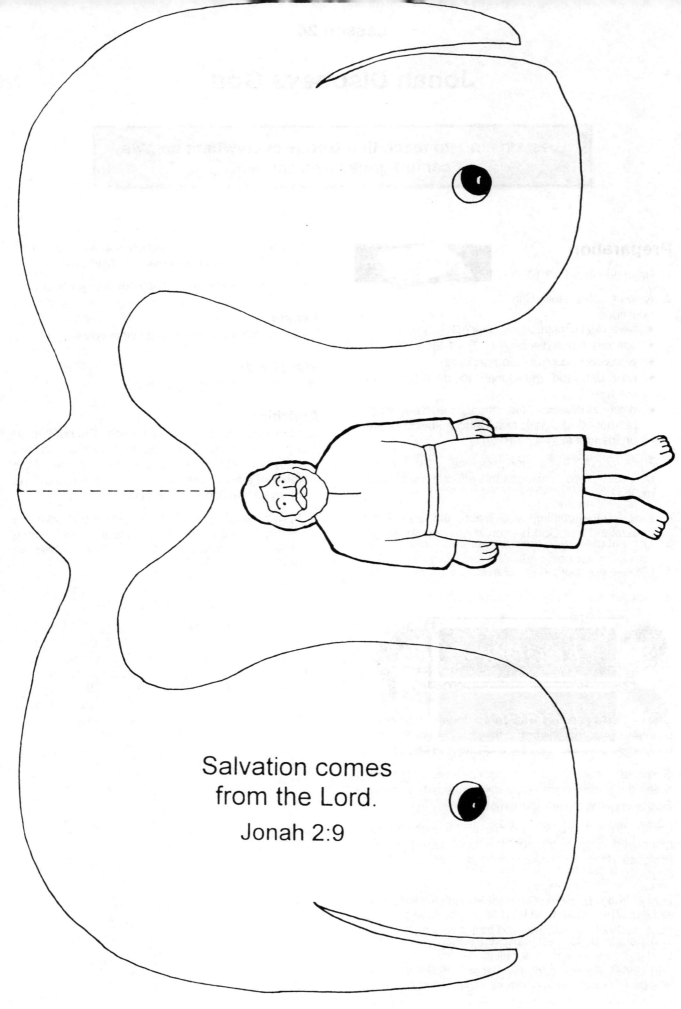

Salvation comes
from the Lord.
Jonah 2:9

Jonah Obeys God

> **Lesson aim: to teach that God forgives those who are truly sorry.**

Preparation

1. Read Jonah 3:1 - 4:11.

2. Answer the following questions:
   - had God's instructions changed? (3:1-2, cf. 1:1-2)
   - did Jonah do what God said? (3:3-4)
   - how did the Ninevites react to Jonah's message? (3:5-9)
   - did God treat the Ninevites as they deserved? (3:10) What does this teach about God's character? (4:2)
   - why was Jonah angry that Nineveh had been spared? (4:1-3) (Nineveh was the capital of Assyria. The Assyrians were cruel people and Israel's enemies.)
   - was Jonah right to be angry?

3. Think about God's great compassion and mercy. Thank him for being willing to forgive all those who truly repent.

4. Pray for the children you teach, that they may turn to God for forgiveness.

5. Choose appropriate visual aids.

Go over the previous lesson on Jonah (1:1 - 2:10).

After 3 days the fish spat Jonah out onto the beach. Again God told Jonah to go to Nineveh and warn them that God would punish them for being so wicked. This time Jonah did what God said. He went to Nineveh and told them that God had seen all the wicked things they were doing. This made God very angry. In 40 days time God would punish the people of Nineveh.

The people of Nineveh believed Jonah. They told God that they were sorry for all the wicked things they had done and stopped doing them. God saw that they were truly sorry so he forgave the people of Nineveh and did not punish them.

Jonah sat outside the city of Nineveh to see if God would destroy it. When God did not destroy the city Jonah was very angry. He did not want God to forgive his enemies. God showed Jonah that he was wrong to be angry. God cares for everyone and forgives everyone who is truly sorry for doing wrong and stops doing it.

Prayer
Dear God, thank you that you forgive everyone who is truly sorry. Amen.

Visual aids
Pictures from a Child's Story Bible.

Activities

1. Discuss with the children the concept of forgiveness - our parents forgive us,
   God forgives us,
   the need to be sorry,
   who should we forgive?

2. Make a story box. Photocopy page 37 on card for each child, having changed the Bible verse to read, *'If we confess our sins, God will forgive us. 1 John 1:9.'* Photocopy page 68 on paper for each child. Make up the boxes following the instructions on page 37. Cut out the 4 pictures from page 68 and place in an envelope for each child.
   The children colour the pictures and glue them in order around the box.
   Use the story box to revise the story.

God told Jonah to go to Nineveh and tell them God was going to punish them for their wicked deeds.

Jonah did what God said.

The people of Nineveh believed Jonah They told God they were sorry. They stopped doing wicked things.

God forgave the people of Nineveh. He did not punish them as he said he would.

Lesson 26

Elijah and the Prophets of Baal

Lesson aim: to teach that God alone is to be worshipped.

Preparation

1. Read 1 Kings 18:1-8,16-39.

2. Answer the following questions:
   - why did Ahab call Elijah the troubler of Israel? (17:1, 18:1-2)
   - who was the real troubler of Israel and why? (v.18)
   - what was Israel's sin? (v.21)
   - what preparations did Elijah make? (v.30-35)
   - what was the reason for the miracle? (v.36-37)
   - what was the result? (v.39)

3. Think about the people's response in v.39. Are you worshipping God alone?

4. Pray for the children, asking God to help you teach this important lesson.

5. Choose appropriate visual aids.

Remind the children of the previous lesson about Elijah (lesson 20).

Three years had passed since Elijah told king Ahab there would be no rain. The ground was very dry and there was not enough grass for the animals to eat. God told Elijah to go to King Ahab and tell him that God would send rain.

When Ahab saw Elijah he said, *'You are the worst troublemaker in Israel.'* Elijah answered, *'No I'm not, you are. You disobeyed God and worshipped Baal. Tell all the people to come to Mount Carmel with all the prophets of Baal.'*

When everyone was at Mount Carmel Elijah said, *'How much longer will it take you to make up your minds whom to worship? If Baal is god, worship him. But if the Lord is God, worship him.'* Then Elijah said they would have a contest. The prophets of Baal would build an altar and he would build another.

Wood and a bull cut up for a sacrifice would be placed on each altar. (You may need to explain sacrifice.) The God who sent fire to burn up the sacrifice would be the real God.

The prophets of Baal went first. They prayed to Baal to send fire, but nothing happened. They kept on asking Baal to send fire, but no fire came. This went on all day. Elijah made fun of them and they called even louder - but nothing happened. No fire came down to burn up the sacrifice.

Then it was Elijah's turn. Elijah took 12 stones and made an altar. He dug a trench round the altar and placed the wood and cut up bull on top. Then he told the people to pour 4 big jugs of water over the bull, wood and altar. The people did this 3 times, until the trench was full of water. Then Elijah prayed to God and asked him to send fire so that the people would know that he was the real God. Straight away God sent fire from heaven and burnt up everything - the sacrifice, the wood, the stones and the water from the trench.

Then all the people said, *'The Lord alone is God!'* and they fell down on their faces and worshipped him.

Stress the lesson aim at this point.

Prayer
Dear God, please help us to worship only you. Amen.

Visual aids
Pictures from a Child's Story Bible.

Activities
1. Photocopy page 70 for each child. Cut out flames from red paper and place in an envelope for each child. The children colour the picture and glue the flames onto the altar.

2. Make a pendant. Photocopy page 71 on card for each child. Cut out the 2 circles and glue them together so that there is a picture on both sides. Make a hole at X using a hole punch. Thread a piece of wool through the hole and join at the ends. The wool loop must be big enough to go over the child's head.

God listened to Elijah's prayer. He sent fire to burn up the sacrifice.

The Lord alone is God.   1 Kings 18:39

Elijah Pendant

God heard Elijah's prayer.

Elijah prayed to God.

The Plagues of Egypt

Lesson aim: to teach that God is powerful and mighty.

Preparation

1. Read Exodus 5:1 - 10:29.

2. Answer the following questions:
   - why did God harden Pharaoh's heart so that he refused to let the Israelites go? (5:2; 6:1,6-8; 7:1-5)
   - list the 10 plagues. Which ones were reproduced by Pharaoh's magicians?
   - which plagues affected Israelites and Egyptians and which ones affected Egyptians only?
   - why were the plagues announced beforehand? (9:1-21)

3. Pray for the children you teach, asking God to help you tell the story clearly and simply.

4. Choose and prepare appropriate visual aids.

Remind the children of the previous 2 weeks' lessons - Moses in the reeds and Moses at the burning bush.

Moses and Aaron went to the king of Egypt and asked him to let the Israelites go so they could serve God. The king said, 'No!', and made the Israelites work even harder. So God told Moses to take his rod and strike the river. Moses did so, and all the water in Egypt turned into blood. All the fish died and the people had nothing to drink. The king asked his magicians if they could do the same, and they could. So the king would not listen to Moses.

A week later Moses went to the king again and asked him to let the Israelites go so they could serve God. Again the king said, 'No!'. So God sent lots of frogs. The frogs got everywhere - in the houses, on the people, even into the cooking pots! And do you know what the king did? He asked his magicians to do the same. So there were even more frogs! But the king still wouldn't let God's people go.

God did many more wonderful things through Moses. He sent gnats, and flies. He sent a disease that killed all the cows, and boils that covered all the people; and each time the king said he would let the people go if only Moses would ask God to stop it. But each time the trouble stopped the king changed his mind and would not let the Israelites go.

So God sent a terrible hail storm and all the people and animals that were outside were killed. But still the king wouldn't let the Israelites go. Then God sent locusts to eat all the plants and darkness that lasted for 3 days. But still the king would not let the Israelites go.

At last God said he would send one final trouble on Egypt, which we will hear about next time.

Prayer
Dear God, there is no-one more powerful than you. Please help us to do what you tell us in your word, the Bible. Amen.

Visual aids
Pictures from a Child's Story Bible.
The pictures on page 73 can be coloured and glued onto squares of card ready to be pinned up on the board at the appropriate point.

Activities
1. Photocopy page 73 for each child. The children colour the picture.

2. Photocopy page 74 x 2 on card for each child and one set for the teacher. Prior to the lesson cut out the 18 cards and place in an envelope for each child. Cut out and colour a set for the teacher. (NB colour matching cards the same.)
   Show the children the set of coloured cards. Place the cards face downwards on the table and mix them up. The children take it in turns to turn over 2 cards to try and find a matching pair. If a pair is found the child keeps the pair and has another turn. If a pair is not found the cards are replaced face down. The winner is the child with most pairs at the end of the game.
   Use the game as a means of revising the story. As each card is turned over ask the children which plague it represents.
   After the game the children can colour their own set of cards.

The Plagues of Egypt (Exodus 5:1 - 10:29)

1. water into blood

2. frogs

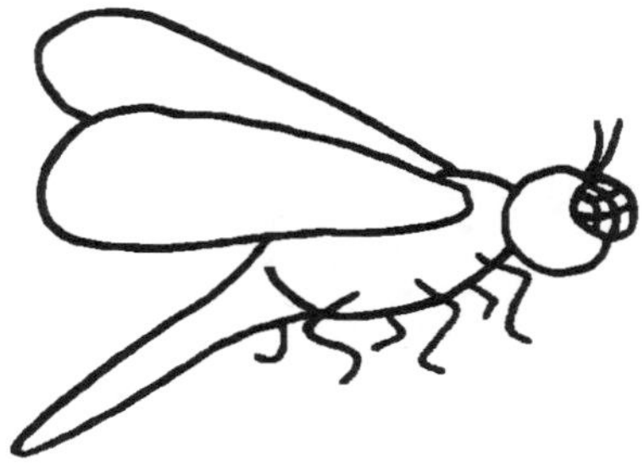

3. gnats

4. flies

5. animal disease

6. boils

7. hail

8. locusts

9. Darkness

God said, "I am the Lord your God." Exodus 6:7

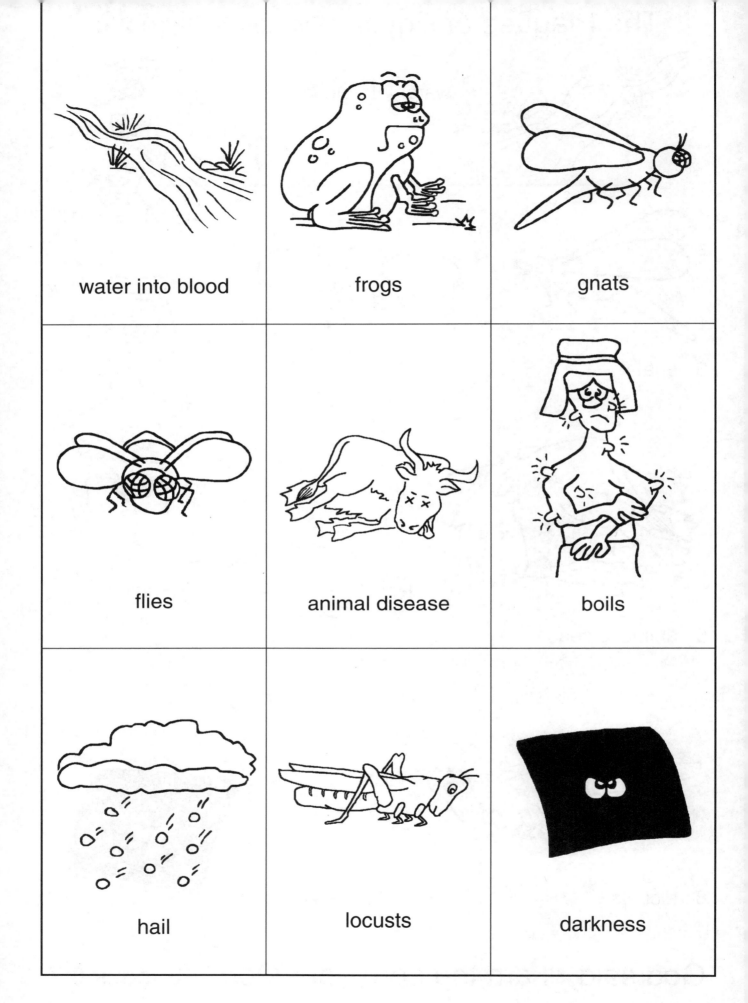

water into blood

frogs

gnats

flies

animal disease

boils

hail

locusts

darkness

The Passover

> **Lesson aim: to teach that God is a saving God.**

Preparation

1. Read Exodus 11:1 - 12:36.

2. Answer the following questions:
   - when had God first told Moses that the Israelites were to ask their neighbours for their valuables? (11:2-3; 3:21-22)
   - God gave specific instructions that his people had to follow if they were to escape the final plague. What were they? (12:3-11,21-23)
   - how does the Passover point forward to the crucifixion? (see also John 1:29, 1 Corinthians 5:7)

3. Think about the way God saved his people from Egypt, and how he saves us through the death and resurrection of Jesus. Think about the great love that made our salvation possible.

4. Pray for the children you teach, that God will use your words to open their eyes to his saving love.

5. Choose and prepare visual aids.

Remind the children of the previous lessons about Moses. Go over what they have learned about God. Use the pictures from page 73 as a reminder of the plagues. If you have not used the lesson on the Plagues of Egypt (OT1) start the story with the following paragraph.

When Moses and Aaron asked the king to let God's people go the king said, *"No!"* So God made lots of bad things happen in Egypt. *(Tell the children about a couple of the plagues.)* Each time something bad happened the king promised to let God's people go. As soon as God took away the *(frogs, hail, etc.)* the king changed his mind and refused to let the people go.

The king still refused to obey God. So God sent Moses to tell the king that the oldest child of every family in Egypt would die at midnight.

But what would happen to the children of God's people, the Israelites? They were also living in Egypt. God arranged a way of escape and sent Moses to tell his people what to do. And this is what they did. Each family got ready to leave. They packed their bags and got dressed for a long journey. Then they took a lamb and killed it and roasted it for their evening meal. Some of the lamb's blood was painted onto the posts on either side of the front door. No-one left their house all night.

That night, when God passed through Egypt to punish the king just as he had promised, he passed over all those houses that had the blood on the door posts and all the children in those houses were saved. (Stress that the people who believed God and did what he told them were saved.) But the king and all his people cried and were sad, because their children were dead.

Then the king told Moses to take the Israelites and all their belongings away from Egypt. This is how God rescued his people from slavery in Egypt, just as he had promised Moses when he spoke to him from the burning bush.

At the end of the story you might want to remind the children of the Easter story and the way God saves his people today.

Prayer
Dear God, thank you saving your people from Egypt. Thank you for Jesus dying on the cross to save us today. Amen.

Visual aids
Pictures from a Child's Story Bible. Pictures of the plagues (pages 73 and 76). You can also use today's activity (pages 76 and 77) as a visual aid.

Activities
1. Photocopy pages 76 and 77 for each child. Prior to the lesson cut out the family from page 76. The children colour the family and glue inside the door posts on page 77. Mark the door posts and lintel with a red crayon to represent blood.

2. Make a cone figure of Moses. Photocopy page 49 on card for each child. Prior to the lesson cut out the appropriate pieces and place in an envelope for each child.

The children colour the pieces. Help them fold the body into a cone shape and glue it together. Place the head on the body by placing the long tab through the hole at the top of the cone. Staple or glue the base of the tab to the inside of the body front. Glue on the head-dress. Glue on cotton wool for a beard.

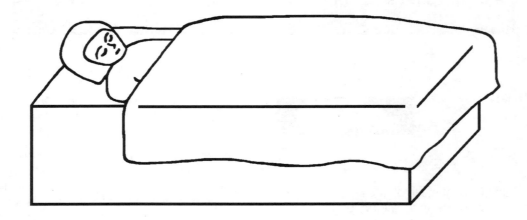

10. death of the first born

God said: "When I see the blood, I will pass over you." Exodus 12:13

Visual aids

Yoghurt Pot People

Requirements

Yoghurt pots or plastic drinking cups, egg cartons, scraps of material, wool, rubber bands, cotton wool, sellotape, glue, pens.

Instructions

Cut the head from an egg carton and sellotape onto a yoghurt pot or plastic cup. Draw on a face. Dress with a piece of material secured round the middle with wool or a rubber band. Tuck the bottom edge of the material inside the bottom of the pot. Attach the head-dress in similar fashion to the robe. Glue on cotton wool as a beard if required.

Peg People

Requirements

Wooden clothes pegs, scraps of material, pink or white paper, card, bluetak, pipe cleaners, cotton wool, needle and thread, glue, pens.

Instructions

1. Wind a piece of paper around the top of the clothes peg and draw on a face.

2. Wrap a pipe cleaner around the peg just below the face and make a loop at each end for the hands.

3. Cut out a length of material twice the length of the peg and approximately 5 cm wide. Make a slit at the centre big enough to go over the top of the peg. Place the material over the top of the peg (see diagram).

4. Wrap the material round the peg and use ½ a pipe cleaner as a belt.

5. Make card feet (see diagram) and attach to the base of the peg with bluetak.

6. Take a square of material approximately 6 x 6 cm to make the head-dress. For a man, attach the head-dress using ½ a pipe cleaner as a head band. For a woman, turn in the top edge of the material then wrap it round the face, securing it with a stitch.

card feet

Finger Puppets

Instructions

1. Using the templates (see below), cut out a body and arms. Draw on a face, head-dress, clothes and hands and colour appropriately. The arms and hands should be coloured on both sides.

2. Roll the body into a tube and glue the back together along the dotted area.

3. Glue the arms onto the back of the body (see diagram).

Playdough

Ingredients   2 cups plain flour
2 cups water
1 cup salt
2 dessert spoons cooking oil
2 oz cream of tartar
food colouring

Mix all the ingredients together in a large saucepan and cook over a low heat, stirring constantly, until the mixture forms a stiff dough. This takes 5 - 10 minutes. Turn the dough out onto a board or work top and knead until the dough is easily malleable. Wrap the dough in cling film and leave to cool. Periodically take the dough out of cling film and knead to remove the crust that forms as it cools. Once the dough is cold give it a final knead and replace in fresh cling film. The dough can be stored wrapped in cling film in an airtight container, e.g. ice cream container, for up to 6 months.